solution-focused
coaching

SOLUTION-FOCUSED COACHING

managing people
in a complex world

Jane Greene
and Anthony M Grant PhD

www.yourmomentum.com
the stuff that drives you

managers

Manager's momentum – a new suite of management development books for the leaders of the future

We've taken the successful approach of the momentum personal development books – active personal coaching, applied personal values and highly stimulating delivery – and applied it to the portfolio of skills that talented leaders of the future will want and need. The result? A set of books and accelerated learning tools for smart managers that will equip you for a bright future of managing talented people and entrepreneurial ventures.

These are intelligent, inspiring yet practical books on a new breed of essential managerial topics – a far cry from an older style of management book, which too often features the same old tired subjects drowned in dense text. Manager's momentum is characterized by edgy, modern subjects delivered in an easily absorbed dynamic style. These are books to make you energized, not tired. And books that you'll be happy to be seen with.

Other manager's momentum titles:
Managing talented people
getting on with – and getting the best from – your high performers
Alan Robertson and Graham Abbey

Also available – momentum personal development books for the stuff that drives you.
Lead yourself
be where others will follow
Mick Cope

Change activist
make big things happen fast
Carmel McConnell

Innervation
personal training for life and work
Guy Browning

The complete list of momentum personal development titles is available via
www.yourmomentum.com

momentum prescription – Let Us Help You Work Out Which Book Will Suit Your Symptoms

Feel stuck in a rut? Something wrong and need help doing something about it?

◆ If you need tools to help make changes in your life: **coach yourself** (a good general guide to change)

◆ If you are considering dramatic career change: **snap, crackle or stop**

◆ If you need to work out what you'd like to be doing and how to get there: **be your own career consultant**

◆ If you need help making things happen and tackling the 'system' at work/in life: **change activist**

◆ If you think you want more from your life than a 'normal' career: **careers un-ltd**

Feel that you can never make decisions and you just let things 'happen'?

◆ If you need help making choices: **the big difference**

◆ If you want to feel empowered and start making things happen for yourself: **change activist**

Feel life is too complicated and overwhelming?

◆ If you need help working through office politics and complexity: **clued up**

◆ If you need a kick up the backside to get out of your commerce-induced coma: **change activist**

◆ If you need an amusing and very helpful modern life survival guide: **innervation**

◆ If you never have enough time or energy to get things done or think properly: **mental space**

Feel like you might be in the wrong job?

◆ If you want help finding your destiny job and inspiration to make that dramatic career change: **snap, crackle or stop**

◆ If you feel like you aren't doing a job that is really what you are about: **soultrader**

◆ If you are struggling with the 'do something worthwhile OR make money dilemma': **change activist**

◆ If you think you want more from your life than a 'normal' career: **careers un-ltd**

Feel that you're not the person/leader you should be?

◆ If you want to be the kind of person others want to follow: **lead yourself**

◆ If you feel your working relationships with people could improve: **managing yourself**

◆ If you need help becoming the person you've always wanted to be: **reinvent yourself**

◆ If you want to work out everything you've got to offer, and how to improve that: **grow your personal capital**

Feel you need help getting your ideas into action?

◆ If the problem is mainly other people, lack of time and the messiness of life: **clued up**

◆ If the problem is communicating your thinking: **hey you!**

◆ If the problem is getting things across to other people: **managing yourself**

◆ If the problem is more ideas than time and you are a bit overwhelmed with work: **mental space**

◆ If the problem is making change in your life: **coach yourself**

Feel you aren't projecting yourself and managing your career as well as you should?

◆ If you'd like to be the kind of person people think of first: **managing brand me**

◆ If you'd like people to listen to your ideas more readily: **hey you!**

◆ If you'd like to come across as the person you really are inside: **soultrader**

◆ If you need general help in changing the way you work/live: **coach yourself**

◆ If you need help working out what you've got and how best to use it: **float you**

Feel you'd like to be much more creative and a real 'ideas person'

◆ If you need inspiration on how to be innovative and think creatively: **innervation**

◆ If you need help spreading your ideas and engendering support: **hey you!**

PEARSON EDUCATION LIMITED

Head Office
Edinburgh Gate
Harlow CM20 2JE
Tel: +44 (0)1279 623623
Fax: +44 (0)1279 431059
Website: www.yourmomentum.com

First published in Great Britain in 2003

The rights of Jane Greene and Anthony Grant to be identified as Authors of this Work has been asserted by them in accordance with the Copyright, Designs and Patents Act 1988.

ISBN 184304028 X

British Library Cataloguing in Publication Data
A CIP catalogue record for this book can be obtained from the British Library.

10 9 8 7 6 5 4 3 2

Typeset by Northern Phototypesetting Co. Ltd, Bolton
Printed and bound in Great Britain by Henry Ling Ltd, Dorchester

The Publishers' policy is to use paper manufactured from sustainable forests.

Dedication

For Georgie, Ben, Toby, Lennart, Leo and Stanley.

Thank you...

We would both like to thank our families and friends for their help and support and our editor, Rachael Stock. We would also like to thank Michael Cavanagh, Deputy Director of the Coaching Psychology Unit for his insight, suggestions and support.

During the course of the research for this book we have talked to many people. We would like to thank them all for their help. In particular: Nick Ayton, Stevan Bennett, David Bell, Gordon Cairns, Kay Cluely, Rod Corban, Ian Coster, Tony Crean, Diane Donaldson, Peter Hammond, Susan Hogg, Ian Hughes, Robert Kaminsky, Daniel King, Charlotte Rastan, Gary Reason, Joanna Reynolds, Kate Roberts, Keith Steele, Christine Turner, Julia Willison, Alan Yentob.

Tony would also like to thank his students at the Coaching Psychology Department, University of Sydney and his clients from his coaching practice.

contents

introduction

what is coaching

Coaching is a collaborative, solution-focused, result-orientated and systematic process in which the coach facilitates the enhancement of work performance, life experience, self-directed learning and personal growth of individuals from normal (i.e., non-clinical) populations.

Anthony M Grant

I cannot teach anybody anything. I can only make them think.

Sooratoo (170BC-399BC) Greek philosopher

Coaching is about creating positive directed change. It is about helping people to develop their potential. Managers can use coaching to enhance and increase the performance of individuals and teams.

One of the most powerful things about coaching is that it works at the level of the individual. An organization cannot exist without people. It can exist without premises, without computers, without products, but not without people. Investing and taking care of people so that you get the best out of them makes commercial and business sense.

Organizations learn only through individuals who learn.

Peter Senge, MIT

An organization is not simply a group of individuals. It is a network of connections, allegiances and relationships. Technological advances, in particular the internet and mobile communications, mean that this web of interactions is increasingly complex. Geographical location doesn't matter much any more in terms of who you work with. You might be part of a work team that includes a sales team in London, IT experts in Frankfurt, business thought leaders in New Jersey, technical experts in Sydney and clients in Stockholm. As a manager you might be the one who has to hold this team together.

Coaching is about creating positive directed change. It is about helping people to develop their potential. Managers can use coaching to enhance and increase the performance of individuals and teams.

An organization is a dynamic system. It is a growing, changing group of people and connections. Patterns emerge, the shape changes; only one thing is certain, it cannot remain the same. And the rate of change is increasing. Even if our predictions and forecasts are accurate today, they may not apply at all tomorrow.

Modern science shows us that more information does not necessarily mean more accurate prediction. With so much data at our disposal it is tempting to feel that if only we can gather more information, exert more control, we can rely on getting the outcomes we want. But things don't necessarily work that way. We want to be able to say if we do X, Y and Z then A, B and C will definitely happen. But this is not true.

An organization is a dynamic system. It is a growing, changing group of people and connections. Patterns emerge, the shape changes only one thing is certain, it cannot remain the same.

We cannot be sure which events will have the greatest impact on the team, the department or the organization. We have to be flexible, sensitive and ready to change. This is one reason why a rigid, top-down management approach is so fraught with difficulty.[1] Reactions times are just too slow. The whole system is too cumbersome.

As a manager *you* are responsible, it is your neck on the block. You have to be in control. How do you manage this contradiction? On the one hand, you are responsible, you have to deliver; on the other hand, you have to let go and allow your team to do the work they are employed to do. There is no easy answer to this conundrum. There is no panacea and, of course, coaching is not the whole answer. It is, however, a powerful tool that you can use to help you to manage people and organizations in today's complex and ever shifting environment.

Successful coaching works on finding solutions. It looks forwards not backwards. It asks 'How can we change this?' and 'How can we do it better?' not 'Why did it happen and who's to blame?'

In one sense, a coaching style of management is a state of mind, an attitude, a shift in perspective. You have to move from the mindset of telling to the mindset of asking. But to make coaching work we need more than just an attitude. We need skills, techniques and models that we can use in a practical way. You need to learn how to let go of telling people what to do and learn ways of asking the right kind of questions of yourself, of your team, of your department. You need to use solution-focused questions that will get the results you need.

In one sense, a coaching style of management is a state of mind, an attitude, a shift in perspective. You have to move from the mindset of telling to the mindset of asking. But to make coaching work we need more than just an attitude.

If you can incorporate solution-focused techniques into your management style you will begin to find that you spend less time unravelling problems and more time leading your team forward in the direction you want to go.

about this book

In this book we take a brief look at where coaching has come from and why it is so important in today's environment. We present the idea of working from a solution-focused perspective and examine specific coaching tools and techniques that have been proven to benefit not only the organization but also the individual.

01

chapter one
why coaching? why now?

A changing world

We need coaching now because the way we work is changing. Most of us have a huge reluctance to change. We would like to preserve the status quo and stay with what we know. But the world is changing fast and organizations are finding that they have to adopt a coaching style of management if they are to remain competitive.

> An International Coach Federation survey of 4000 companies found that the reported benefits of coaching included:
>
> ◆ improved individual performance
>
> ◆ improved profit, client service and competitiveness
>
> ◆ development of people for the next level
>
> ◆ management/staff relationship improvement
>
> ◆ improved retention.
>
> *Training and Development*, February 2000

Coaching enhances emotional intelligence, i.e. the ability to understand and use our emotions in a constructive way.

We've identified that the key success factor in performance improvement is leadership and the key success factor in leadership improvement is to be self-aware – to have strong emotional intelligence. Gordon Cairns, CEO, Lion Nathan, speaking on TV

We need coaching now because the way we work is changing. Most of us have a huge reluctance to change. We would like to preserve the status quo and stay with what we know.

Although, traditionally, IQ has been seen to be the most powerful predictor of success,[1] recent work with emotional intelligence and coaching indicates that long-term success requires much more than sheer rational thinking power. We all know of the very bright person who, although technically superb at their work, always seems to be putting other people's backs up – indeed, poor interpersonal and intrapersonal skills are the key executive derailers.[2]

Many organizations now provide coaches to their high fliers as part of their professional development.

I was brought in to start a new department. It was something new to the organization and everyone had great hopes for it. It was quite a big department on both sides of the Atlantic. Also, it was a very bureaucratic organization, just because it was so big. I was in quite a senior position so, after about a year, my boss suggested I go to a management coach. I was sort of supposed to be a high flier and he wanted me to go a really long way and go far. He thought this would help me find my way through the intricacies of the organization.   Susanna, scientist

But as well as providing outside coaches for top players, companies are finding that there can be enormous benefits in training managers to be workplace coaches. These include:[3]

◆ better communication

◆ less conflict

◆ greater cooperation

◆ increased self-awareness

◆ overall better performance

◆ reduced staff turnover

◆ shared vision and commitment.

pages 2 / 3

chapter one

solution-focused coaching

momentum

Information overload

Oceans of information are now available to anyone who has access to a personal computer and the internet. As a manager what you need is people who can access, interpret and use this information. For modern organizations attraction and retention of the best people is more crucial than ever.

We need to learn to share, sort and synthesize information, rather than just direct the work of others.

Kenichi Ohmae, *Business Minds*, p.180

Knowledge is now a vital commodity. The knowledge inside workers' heads is a crucial and often primary asset of many modern organizations.

The knowledge in people's heads is crucial. I will employ people for the knowledge in their heads as much as for their skills.

Joanna Reynolds, MD, Time Life Europe

But knowledge quickly becomes redundant. To be successful, organizations need people who can quickly learn and adapt to new situations.

All of our businesses have in common that constant refreshing, doing it again. You produce a book that goes to the top of the best seller lists but it's already yesterday's news. That process is getting quicker and quicker and it's getting more and more difficult for people to deal with.

David Bell, Director of People, Pearson

The old models

We are moving from an industrial era where wealth lay in raw materials, machinery, goods – what Karl Marx called 'the means of production' – into a world where wealth and power lie in ideas, imagination, knowledge and the information you control.

Some of the richest and most powerful organizations on earth do not produce any tangible goods at all. For example, as Naomi Klein points out in her book, *No Logo*, sportswear giant Tommy Hilfiger doesn't manufacture anything at all. The whole multimillion-dollar organization is run through licensing agreements.

Scientific management

At the beginning of the 20th century the concept of scientific management was created by industrialist F. W. Taylor. Taylor believed that each task could be broken down into its component parts. He believed in clear lines of command. In a sense he wanted to turn every organization into an efficient machine. He developed his ideas at a time when, in order to be successful, companies needed to produce more goods, more efficiently. Taylor's ideas, which were hugely influential, still persist today, although many people have forgotten or perhaps never knew where they came from. But we are moving out of the industrial age. Even for companies that do produce 'things', the value lies less in the objects themselves and more in the brand image, relationships and ideas.

We are moving out of the industrial age. Even for companies that do produce 'things', the value lies less in the objects themselves and more in the brand image, relationships and ideas.

In our new age being elusive is good. If you can touch something it is probably not worth a great deal. What is valuable at Volvo . . . you cannot touch . . . What is valuable is the intangible – the Volvo brand, the relationships, the knowledge that exists within the company, the concepts and the ideas.

Funky Business, p 95

What most organizations want and need now are talented, creative individuals. The main aim of scientific management was to iron out individual differences. Now it is those differences, that very creativity that we need. Today we don't need people to be machines. We have machines to be machines. We need people to think, learn and interpret and use the information that is available to us. We need individuals.

It is increasingly true that companies are successful not because they have the best equipment, the best technology, the largest number of employees, but because they have the best people, working in the best way.

The post-bureaucratic organization requires a new kind of partnership between leaders and the led. Today's organizations are evolving into federations, networks, clusters, cross-functional teams, temporary systems, ad hoc task forces, lattices, modules, matrices – almost anything but pyramids with their obsolete top-down leadership.

Warren Bennis, academic, author, government advisor

Competitive advantage is a subtle and shifting concept. It is hard to predict with any certainty who will gain it and how they might do it. What is certain is that, in order to understand and interpret the complex world we live in, organizations need people who can decipher information, make connections, see patterns, create networks, react quickly and adapt to circumstance.

It is very, very difficult to recruit in our industry. Technical skills you can pick up reasonably easy but they do not translate into the ability of operating as a consultant. So often you might end up perhaps with not the most technically brilliant people but people that can actually translate and operate in the field.

Peter Hammond, company director

Technical competence is not enough. In fact, it has become a baseline requirement, a given. Organizations now need people with a wide range of emotional intelligence, intuition, flexibility and adaptability, on top of their technical skills and competencies. Everyone, every organization now wants and needs the best people and, once they've got them, they need to hold onto them and to get the best out of them.

The talented employee may join a company because of its charismatic leaders, its general benefits, and its world-class training programs, but how long that employee stays and how productive he is while he is there is determined by his relationship with his immediate supervisor. *First Break All the Rules*, p. 12

Today's manager plays a crucial role in retention of staff.

The emergence of the knowledge-based economy requires managers to learn to act as 'coaches'. In a knowledge-based economy, a company must be more innovative to keep up with the accelerated speed of change, and its workforce must acquire the learning skills that will foster innovativeness in the company. Managers can help achieve these goals if they learn how to coach their subordinates ... and not merely manage tasks, but facilitate the functioning of work teams.

HR Focus, January 1996

A conceptual flaw in management thinking is that people are a separate side of management and that strategy belongs in a separate silo. This is completely wrong . . . The way you manage people is the way you manage. Because a company comprises people

Philip Whitely, co-author, *Unshrink*

Social capital

Organizations run better when people know and trust one another. Teams are more productive, deals move faster, people perform better when the relationships that make the organization work effectively are strong.[4] The *social capital* of an organization can be vital to its success. With an increase in electronic communication, many people working off-site, and an increased reliance on contract and freelance workers, social capital is under threat.

If the relationships in an organization are more numerous, varied and fleeting then it is even more important that communication be clear, open and honest. *Integrity, openness* and *trust* are more important than ever. But they are not easy to achieve.

The manager's role is no longer one of simply supervising and
directing. To be effective managers need to extend their skills to
include collaboration and empowerment.[5] Coaching helps them to
do this.

A complex world

The massive computation power of today's computers has changed
the world but not in the way we thought it would. We used to be
afraid that computers would outthink us, even take over (see Stanley
Kubrick's film, *2001*) and for a while this seemed to be coming true.

Some scientists claimed it had come true in 1997 when IBM's
computer Deep Blue beat world chess champion Garry Kasparov.
The victory (disputed by some) was widely hailed as an important
breakthrough for artificial intelligence and was reported in the
world's press, sweeping other news off the front pages. Once chess
was seen as the ultimate intellectual challenge. It was seen as *The
Holy Grail of researchers into Artificial Intelligence* (Daniel King in
'Kasparov v Deeper Blue', Batsford Ltd., 1997, p. 9). But many
commentators dismissed Deep Blue's alleged victory as no more
impressive than any other purely mechanical achievement.

The fact is that, despite our fears, computers still can't think for us
but they are changing our world in ways we didn't quite predict.
Computers allow scientists to carry out calculations that previously
would have been impossible, not because they were too difficult but
because they would have taken too long to complete. This massive
computational power has allowed scientists to develop first chaos
and then complexity theory. These theories show us that when
change comes it can come quickly. Complex systems are webs or

networks where the agents within the system constantly interact. Change in one part of the system can quickly cascade through the whole structure. Complexity also shows us that out of seeming disorder and chaos patterns can begin to emerge.

Complex systems are webs or networks where the agents within the system constantly interact. Change in one part of the system can quickly cascade through the whole structure. Complexity also shows us that out of seeming disorder and chaos patterns can begin to emerge.

Malcolm Gladwell illustrates this phenomenon in his book, *The Tipping Point*. He uses an example from New York. A few 'cool' people started wearing a previously uncool brand of shoes, Hush Puppies. More and more people noticed them and started wearing them too. A pattern is emerging that 'cool people wear Hush Puppies'. Suddenly a huge number of people start wearing them, seemingly all at the same time. A Hush Puppy 'epidemic' is created, seemingly from nowhere. Meanwhile, the original cool people, or even different cool people, have moved onto something else and new patterns emerge.

But perhaps the biggest change in our day-to-day lives is the fact that the widespread use of personal computers is changing the way we communicate.

At this point you may be asking yourself, *What does all this have to do with coaching? How is it going to help me lead my team?* The point is that coaching works at the level of the *individual*. Chaos theory tells us that a tiny change can lead to an enormous effect. So a change at the level of the individual can lead to a change in the whole organization. Like the famous butterfly effect, where the cause of a tornado can be traced back to the flap of a butterfly's wing thousands of miles away. The point is that we can only see the causal patterns in hindsight – we cannot look forward and predict them. There are too many variables. Add to this the fact that the number of variables and interactions has been massively increased by the fact that at the touch of a button any one of us can send a message to thousands, even millions, of people all around the world.

It has been the tendency of business to behave as though, by having a great deal of information and by controlling outcomes very carefully, we will be able to forecast what is going to happen next. But science is showing us that even with the most accurate data we cannot predict the future. So what do we do? How do we manage today's organizations? The answer seems to be that we have to keep trying different things, being flexible and adaptable. We need to be able to feed information back into the system, being prepared to learn, grow and change. We need coaching.

Simple rules

One often-used illustration of complexity theory at work is that of a flock of birds. Flocks of birds move together across the sky, turning and swooping in unison, forming complex patterns. It looks as though their movements are orchestrated, as if they are all following one *leader*. In fact, computer modelling has shown that three simple rules keep the birds flying together as one flock. These rules are:

◆ Fly in the same direction as the bird in front.

◆ Fly at the same speed as the bird in front.

◆ Try not to bump into anything.

This type of phenomenon has been called *distributed control* as opposed to *central control*, where the guy at the top is in charge and leads the way.

Shared values and shared goals engender these kinds of simple rule within an organization. A group of people who have a set of values and goals that are understood and shared strongly simply don't need so much top-down control.

Exercise

Try this simple exercise to demonstrate distributed control in action.

Take a group of people to an open space such as a car park (numbers don't really matter, but to get the best effect you need about 14) and divide them into two groups, A and B. Give group A the rule 'Stand two metres from a B'. Don't tell the Bs this rule. Instead give them the rule 'Stand between two As'. Similarly, don't tell the A group this rule. The groups are not allowed to talk to each other during the exercise.

The individuals in the groups will start walking about, moving around each other. After a while the group will settle into a pattern or a system, with people at specific distances from one another. You can then try experimenting. Move an 'A' a metre or so to the right. The whole group will probably shuffle around. Or they may not quite notice and will stay still. Some movements will affect the whole group, others will not. It is very difficult, if not impossible, to predict how much, if at all, the group will shift.

When you ask people what rule the other group was following, they will come up with things like, *They were trying to communicate with us but they weren't allowed to talk* and other equally creative suggestions.

This exercise was first developed by Michael Cavanagh, at the Coaching Psychology Unit in the University of Sydney, and has been used many times to illustrate the complexity of human systems.

There are three key points that come out of this. First, small changes can lead to large effects – ripples through the group – but sometimes big changes don't have any effect at all. Second, the system works, a pattern emerges even if not everyone understands the rules or works on different rules. Third, when we don't understand the rules we tend to make up rules which explain our experience. (Interestingly, it seems we tend to prefer complex to simple explanations.)

Exercise 2

Gather a group of about ten people. Get them to sit or stand in a circle facing towards the outside of the circle, or to close their eyes so they can't see each other. Simply ask them to start clapping in time with each other.

After a very short time, twenty seconds or so, you will usually notice that the clapping becomes rhythmic. They all tend towards a pattern. But if you leave them to continue clapping, the rhythm will start to change. The rhythm often speeds up and then starts to fragment.

However, it does not take very long before the group starts to clap in time again, even though no one overtly sets the pace. The group takes on a dynamic of its own – it becomes self-organizing.

Sometimes one person deliberately tries to set the pace, or change the rhythm. What is interesting here is that this often leads to a fragmented rhythm, or even a complete breakdown.

This exercise is another powerful metaphor for the limitations of management by command and control. One person trying to purposefully change the system can have disastrous results, whilst someone else who is in tune with the group can be a powerful agent of change.

Again this demonstrates a kind of distributed control and the emergent rhythms are what complexity theory calls 'attractors'.

The key thing in both these experiments is that it is very difficult to predict exactly what will happen. The systems are dynamic and changing. What you put in is not necessarily what you get out.

No more jobs for life

Many people now work from home at least part of the time and freelance and contract work is on the increase. People move jobs frequently. You may be part of several different project and work teams, each one consisting of people who might have a variety of loyalties and tied to a variety of different people and organizations.

Just over 50 years ago, J. Lyons and Co. was one of the biggest catering firms in Britain. Their famous 'corner houses' were a part of British culture and Lyons did *everything* themselves.
They grew their own tea, built their own trucks, even built their own ovens to bake their own kind of Swiss rolls. At J. Lyons everything was in-house – a situation that is completely unthinkable today. (Incidentally, this *we'll do it ourselves* mentality lead to Lyons building and using the first ever business computer system.)

With such massive changes in the way we work, of course, we have to change the way we manage. On the one hand, you are responsible, on the other hand, you must not over-control. But how do we depend on those we don't control? Isn't it too great a risk to take? The temptation can be to try to exert greater and greater control. 'Management by tantrum' is an all too common (if not very successful) approach.

People want to work with you now rather than for you. Those are tiny words but a big distinction. I think the command and control model is probably over. David Bell, Director of People, Pearson

Learning how to use coaching techniques is a way of reconciling these two things. It is a way of allowing people the freedom to use their own experience, talent, skills and resources while, at the same time, setting clear goals and making sure the job gets done.

We are intending to develop the partners to be able to coach rather than just supervise. I would hope that within about, say, two years we would be coaching as naturally as we currently supervise. In a sense I would hope that we don't even really need to talk about 'coaching' anymore – that it just becomes 'the way we do things around here'.
Keith Steele, senior litigation partner and National Head of Coaching for Freehills Commercial Litigation Group (one of the largest corporate law firms in Australia)

Ideally, the coaching mindset needs to go right through the organization. If you work in an organization where the old top-down command and control approach is still predominant you may find it much more difficult to coach.[6] But people increasingly want and expect to work in this more open, egalitarian culture.[7]

I try to coach the people I work with to manage in the way that will get the best out of people and to see that different people have different needs.
Joanna Reynolds, MD, TimeLife Europe

Good management is invisible

Many people who find themselves as managers did not set out to be managers. They started out as lawyers, accountants, teachers, journalists, mechanics, nurses, computer programmers, salespeople, shop assistants, trapeze artists, any number of things. But if you do well at your job you very often find yourself having to take responsibility for other people. For many people the job of managing people is not one they want to think about too much. They just want to get the job done. People are a part of the process and managing them is something you just have to do as part of getting to the end result.

'I'm lucky enough to work with people who don't seem to cause me any real trouble at all', says Lucy Jones, executive producer of a highly successful independent TV production company. She is working with directors, presenters, researchers and actors. She is managing a complex mixture of people, deadlines and budgets. She gets the best out of the people working for her and she chooses them carefully. Because she is a creative and talented manager the projects she works on are successful and people feel good about themselves and her. Trust is built up and success builds on success. Lucy's people don't cause her any trouble, they don't need to because she manages them well. Yet she is hardly aware of doing it. Someone like Lucy is worth a fortune to the company she works for and they are aware of it.

When my first programme came out and the viewing figures were very good the chief executive rang me to congratulate me. I think things like that make a huge difference.

Lucy is valuable not only because of her technical skills but also because of her adaptability, her flexibility and her readiness to learn. Lucy works in the TV industry but all sorts of organization are finding that competitive advantage lies in having the right people working for them: people like Lucy who can get the best out of their teams. Technical skills are no longer enough. Companies need people who are flexible, clear sighted and good learners.

Meaning and purpose are what drive people. The manager coach needs to understand this. The coaching mindset is like the oil that lubricates the relationships between managers and their teams. It provides organizations with a process by which they can enable their employees to grow, change and adapt.

So coaching, developing the potential of the workforce, is important both for the organization and for the individual. Without it the best and the brightest people will move on and those who are left behind will be under-used and undervalued.

Taylor's ideas may have kept great engines of the industrial age turning over but soon after Taylor's scientific management became widespread, science itself changed with the publication of Einstein's theory of relativity. It was not only industry but the whole world that began to seem uncertain.

Our world is constantly adapting and changing and today we need something far more subtle and sophisticated to keep our organizations working efficiently. Coaching is one way in which managers can develop their people's potential and help individuals and organizations reach their goals.

Our goal is to have working for us people who could always leave but decide not to – because the opposite of that is a nightmare.

David Bell, Director for People, Pearson

chapter one

solution-focused coaching

momentum

Where has coaching come from?

Workplace coaching has its roots in:

◆ counselling and therapy

◆ mentoring

◆ training

◆ management consulting.

Coaching borrows from all these disciplines but there are important differences.

Coaching and counselling and therapy

Coaching is *not* therapy but it does use some techniques derived from clinical psychology. Coaching deals with individuals who are functional, often people who are performing very well indeed. Coaching is less about unravelling problems and difficulties and more about building solutions and improving performance.

Coaching and mentoring

Coaching is often confused with mentoring. In fact, sometimes the terms are used interchangeably. There are areas of overlap but there is an important distinction:

◆ A mentor is usually an expert in a particular field and works with more junior practitioners in that field, helping them to gain knowledge, skills and experience.

◆ Coaching is about facilitating self-directed learning and development. The coach does not necessarily have specific expertise in the area of influence of the person he or she is coaching.

Sometimes not having expertise in the working area of a client allows a valuable insight. As one executive coach puts it:

When I come from the position of being the expert, it's almost as if I have to defend my position. But when you say to yourself 'I'm not the expert' even though you may have all this knowledge, it feels more open and you can play around with those ideas. It means I pay more attention. It becomes more active than defensive. It's very powerful.

Coaching and training

Training is about teaching particular skills. It is often a fixed process – a certain number of employees are required to learn a specific set of skills. Unfortunately, the transfer of skills learned on the training course to the workplace tends to be rather low.[8]

Studies have shown that coaching used *in conjunction* with training can make the training much more effective.[9]

Olivero, Bane and Kopelman examined the effects of executive coaching in a public sector municipal agency. Thirty-one managers underwent a managerial training programme, which was followed by eight weeks of one-on-one executive coaching. Training increased productivity by 22.4%. The coaching, which included goal setting, collaborative problem solving, practice, feedback, supervisory involvement, evaluation of end results and a public presentation, increased productivity by 88.0%. This represented a significantly greater gain compared to training alone. Results indicate that executive coaching is an important way of ensuring that knowledge acquired during training actually emerges as skills that are applied to work.

Coaching and management consulting

Consultants tend to be experts in their area. Coaches are experts in facilitating learning and goal attainment. Management consultants are expected to come up with a model for change, based on information gleaned from the current state of the organization. They will tend to go into an organization, suggest a solution and then leave. Coaches help the clients find their own solutions. Management consultants tend to work with information, processes and procedures. Coaches work with individuals, relationships and interpersonal skills. Consultants tell – coaches ask the right questions.

Management consultants tend to work with information, processes and procedures. Coaches work with individuals, relationships and interpersonal skills. Consultants tell – coaches ask the right questions.

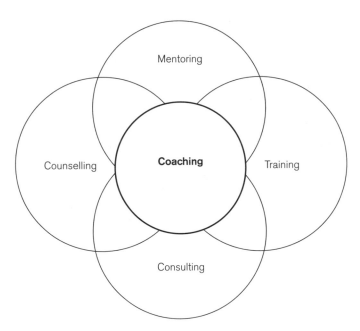

Figure 1.1 The relationship between coaching, counselling, mentoring, training and consulting

chapter two
focusing on solutions

What is solution-focused coaching?

The true scientist is imaginative as well as rational, and sometimes leaps to solutions where reason can follow only slowly.
Isaac Asimov (1920–1992), Russian-born US author

A sure cure for seasickness is to sit under a tree.
Spike Milligan (1918–2002), actor and comedian

Coaching is solution focused. This means it works more on finding answers and less on untangling problems. At one level this is a simple shift of emphasis but it makes an important and profound difference to the way we deal with things.

Most good managers agree that in order to motivate the people working with them they have work at an individual level to construct a shared vision. Good managers are able to promote belief in a shared goal. They have to look forwards, not backwards. They have to focus on solutions.

I sell a vision to my staff. I try to say OK let's look at the big positives in this and what can we do to get the best out of it? There's always an opportunity in it somewhere.
Joanna Reynolds, MD, TimeLife Europe

At its best, solution-focused coaching enables people to access and use the wealth of experience, skills, expertise and intuition that we all have. It allows people to find individual and creative solutions to the situations they find themselves in, both at work and in their personal lives.

At the simplest level focusing on solutions represents a shift of emphasis. But at a more profound level it can mean a complete reframing of the way you look at events and circumstances. Solution-focused thinking can be applied to all sorts of areas of life.

A solution-focused approach means working with some basic principles:

◆ There is always a better way.

◆ There is no failure, only feedback.

◆ The map is not the territory – perceptions and reality often differ.

◆ People are resourceful.

◆ If it works, keep doing it.

◆ Start with small changes.

◆ Build on success.

◆ Flexibility engenders success.

◆ Praise, compliment and acknowledge.

At its best, solution-focused coaching enables people to access and use the wealth of experience, skills, expertise and intuition that we all have. It allows people to find individual and creative solutions to the situations they find themselves in, both at work and in their personal lives.

The solution-focused approach says that when faced with a difficult situation you need to:

◆ clarify goals

◆ decide what you want to change

◆ see the problem as something you have (not are)

◆ focus on times when you have coped

◆ chart your progress towards the solution

◆ clarify the central goal or issue

◆ look at your strengths and successes.

It also means that:

◆ Instead of dwelling on a problem you need to work on finding a solution.

◆ You may need to try several different solutions until you find one that is right for you.

◆ You need to find and use any resources that can help you build solutions.

◆ You need to look at times when you have encountered and dealt with similar problems in the past and dealt with them successfully.

Where has the solution-focused approach come from?

In a sense it hasn't *come from* anywhere. It is a way at looking at situations that many successful people have used for centuries. The solution-focused approach has its roots in:

◆ Milton H. Erickson's work on hypnosis and communication in the late 1950s[1]

◆ cognitive psychology and philosophy

◆ Alfred Korzybski's work on general semantics.

Erickson's work influenced many people and gave rise to a psychotherapy known as brief solution-focused therapy.[2] This approach has been used extensively and with very good result in the fields of education,[3] child behavioural problems,[4] drug counselling[5] and many other areas.

It is based on two very simple premises:

◆ Even the most persistent problem is not present absolutely all the time. There are always some exceptions. For example, if you are depressed there must be some moments that are not as bad as others.

◆ If you know where you are headed it is easy to get there. So, imagining a future helps you to reach it.

Practitioners of solution-focused therapy found that labelling people as sick often perpetuated the problem.[6] Instead, they encouraged them to see themselves as whole and competent individuals. And it seems to work. There is now a growing body of research which shows that brief solution-focused therapy is successful.

The solution-focused approach is a conscious and deliberate approach to changing the way you view situations and circumstances. It is a simple practical approach to problems. Just because it is so practical and simple it is tempting to dismiss this type of thinking as vague or too soft but many organizations are beginning to realize that it is just this type of *soft skills* that are crucial to their success. In fact, the soft skills are often hardest to utilize.

We went to the States and looked at what some of the most financially successful companies were doing. Valuing people and building on successes. Acknowledging and valuing what they did well was without question a critical variable for success in every single company we talked to.

Alan Yentob, Director of Drama, Entertainment and Children's Programmes, BBC

Example

A TV production company that has enjoyed a great deal of success is finding that the commissions are not coming in. There is unhappiness and discontent within the organization. Everyone feels that things are not working out.

The executive realize that they need to look at their management practices.

The problem-focused approach

They decide to look into the exact causes of discontent and try to isolate who and what is causing it, if necessary looking at getting rid of anyone who is not pulling their weight.

The solution-focused approach

They get together to take a look at the sort of programmes they *want* to be making and to decide what personal values are important to the people working in the company. The one thing they all agree on is that they want to make excellent, cutting-edge programmes.

They also look back at past successes and try to identify the things they do well. Each employee is asked to write down a list of the work they feel most proud of. In this way each person begins to feel that they are part of a company that has achieved great things in the past and that is committed to excellence and creativity.

With this information they can start to build a shared vision for the future of the company.

Why does the solution-focused approach work?

This approach works because it works at the level of the individual 'agent' in the system. It is a *bottom-up* rather than a *top-down* way of working.

Example

The Defence Aviation Repair Agency (DARA), based in South Wales, has done a lot of work on linking people issues with its overall strategy goals. They called in management consultants to help them streamline their processes. However, it was not until they started to use a facilitator who worked *directly* with the engineers on the shop floor that they started to see real changes, Chief Executive Steve Hill said, speaking on BBC's current affairs programme *Newsnight*. They then got the *engineers themselves* to look at the processes and make time-saving changes where they could.

It used to take us 52 weeks to turn round a main rotor gearbox for a Lynx helicopter. Top down we drove it to 13 weeks. The guys themselves drove it down to 16 days.

This seems incredible but it's true. In fact, DARA has won several industry awards for good management practice. They have flattened their management structure moving from a very command and control structure to one where the work teams themselves have a good deal of control over working practices.

Looking for causes

In the western world, we like to look for causes to our problems. It is ingrained in our mindset, it is almost like our lifeblood. It is the way we see things. We feel that if we go into all the possible details of what may have caused a problem, we will be able to solve it. Often we seem to believe that we cannot even begin to build a solution until we fully understand what has gone wrong before. Science is now beginning to show us that understanding causes does not always allow us to predict effects. Chaos theory and complexity theory highlight the fact that sometimes very small changes can produce huge effects.

In the western world, we like to look for causes to our problems. It is ingrained in our mindset, it is almost like our lifeblood. It is the way we see things. We feel that if we go into all the possible details of what may have caused a problem, we will be able to solve it.

This is why the solution-focused approach is so important. Focusing on solutions means that you use the solutions that are happening *anyway* and build on these. Working from the individual's perspective means that managers can capitalize on patterns that are emerging and use them to move the organization and their team forward. This is a powerful organic and dynamic way to move forward.

By dwelling on the causes of problems we often perpetuate and exaggerate them. Over-engaging in self-reflection and focusing on problems actually makes us feel worse.[7] By looking for solutions we immediately shift the emphasis from the past to the future. From *why* to *how to*. Sometimes, the how to question can be answered by noticing what's already working and doing more of that.

Example

A woman in her late 20s, working as a stockbroker, decided she needed help from a coach. She had a very successful career in what is traditionally a male-dominated environment. Her working day was spent in a very aggressive atmosphere. A lot of shouting and abuse went on – and although she was very successful and was making a lot of money, she found the culture that she was working in very stressful. Her male colleagues did not always treat her very well. She was thinking about changing career altogether. Despite a master's degree and years of experience she had had enough. She wanted help from the coach in deciding what to do next in her career.

At first the coach was not sure what to suggest. A traditional counselling approach would be to listen, to empathize and to acknowledge how stressful and to validate how difficult it must feel. However, using solution-focused techniques what the coach actually said to her was this.

'You've been working in this environment for two years. How have you managed to cope so well?'

At first the woman looked stunned. Then her body language changed. From looking subdued and miserable and like a victim she immediately straightened up. She thought about it and explained that the tension built up, until every six weeks or so she exploded and had a massive row with her boss. He would listen to her complaints, while she vented her anger, and then he persuaded her to stay on in the company. For a while afterwards she felt better, until the tension built up to an unbearable level once again.

At a loss as to what to suggest, the coach drew on the core solution-focused principles. Using the 'do more of what works' approach, the coach suggested that she try having a row more often. As this is what made her feel better, why didn't she try having a row every two weeks!

The woman was somewhat taken aback by this, but decided to give it a go.

Once every two weeks she approached her boss with issues she needed to talk about. She 'had a row' except, of course, it wasn't a row, it was a meeting, a debrief, a time when she was heard. She let the boss know what she needed and how she felt. Communication between them dramatically improved and over time she was perceived by her colleagues to be much more assertive and in control. As a result of this they began to treat her with more respect and consideration. Over time the culture of the work environment significantly changed.

Coaching is a dialogue between coach and client where they work together to define the issues and jointly construct a solution. By shifting our perspective from what caused the problem to what the solution might look like, we often find that we can move on from seemingly intractable situations.

Experience and intuition

This approach acknowledges that by looking only at what we perceive to be rational, logical and obvious causes we shut ourselves off from a wide range of intuition, knowledge and skills. Perception, intuition, imagination are important resources that we all have at our disposal. We tend not to trust anything other than rational, logical thought, despite the fact that we are emotional, instinctive beings. But we are moving from a very rational age to one where we are beginning to acknowledge that emotion, intuition and perception are important. Our lived experience counts.

Pure logical thinking cannot yield us any knowledge of the empirical world; all knowledge of reality starts from experience and ends in it.

Albert Einstein

It is strange that we mistrust our intuition to such an extent. After all, stripped of the pseudo-mystical, intuition is simply automatic, unconscious access to information that we have acquired over time. Anyone who has developed a skill knows that there are times when intuition and experience take over. In fact, to be really good at many things you have to go beyond rational thought; you have to *trust your intuition*.

Charlie's case study

Charlie is a junior hospital doctor. He is working at a large teaching hospital as a senior house officer in the accident and emergency department. Despite his medical training, on his first day in the department he feels quite overwhelmed by what seems to him the utter chaos that is all around him. There are drunks with gashes to their heads, shouting abuse at the nurses. A breathless old lady in her slippers – children crying, a few homeless people who seem to have wandered in just to keep warm. A man who is insisting loudly that he needs urgent attention, a group of teenagers one of whom seems to be unable to stand up. He has no idea where to begin or how he is going to manage to deal with everything and everyone.

Luckily the nurses are utterly capable and competent and seem quite unfazed by the situation.

Charlie gets through the first shift by relying on the skills and experience of the nurses and more senior doctors. Gradually, over time he begins to get used to being greeted by such an assortment of people and ailments and after a few weeks he can quickly get a fair idea of which cases are serious, who needs to be seen immediately and which illnesses and accidents are most important.

He begins to be able to rely on his experience and intuition to tell him which cases are most serious.

WHAT DOES THE RESEARCH SHOW?

Research carried out with 15 male and female nurses (aged 23–49 years) in Germany showed that nurses with less implicit knowledge rely more on explicit knowledge during critical situations than those with more implicit knowledge.

Implicit and explicit knowledge: Influences on action in critical situations.

Zeitschrift für Psychologie mit Zeitschrift für Angewandte Psychologie,
2001, **209**(2): 174–200, Johann Ambrosius Barth Verlag, Germany

When we are learning to do something we focus a lot of attention on acquiring the skill and developing the confidence we need.[8] Once we have become proficient we can concentrate on other, more subtle aspects. A virtuoso musician has the technical ability and confidence to play almost any piece of music. Little or no thought goes into reading the music, fingering, technique or timing. The entire concentration can be focused on interpretation. We all have masses of implicit knowledge that we never have to think about accessing or using.

The only really valuable thing is intuition.   Einstein

WHAT DOES THE RESEARCH SHOW?

Research at the University of Lancaster has shown that when a football player is under stress the control of his movements change. As he becomes stressed the movements become less variable and less fluid. He begins to move more like a learner.

Rod Corban showed that when you learn a task, when you have to think about your movements, one part of the brain – the vertical stream – is more involved but when you are proficient, and the movements are unconscious, a different part – the dorsal stream – is involved. Anxiety kicks in the vertical stream and movements become more stilted.

This phenomenon is called 'choking'. Anxiety makes the players less able to perform. And so they need to find ways of overcoming or outwitting their anxiety if they are to perform at their best.

By visualizing a successful outcome, sportspeople can manage to overcome this phenomenon.

Collins, D., Jones, B., Fairweather, M., Doolan, S. and Priestley, N. (2001). Examining anxiety associated changes in movements patterns. *International Journal of Sport Psychology*, 31, 223–42.

and

Masters, R. S. W., (2000). Theoretical aspects of implicit learning in sport. *International Journal of Sport Psychology*, 31, 530–41.

Sportspeople, musician, actors, public speakers, chess players, surgeons, in fact people from all walks of life and types of profession have to learn to trust their implicit knowledge. They have to trust themselves to know what they are doing because the minute they start to doubt it, and think too carefully about what they are doing, they are liable to *choke* or fail in their task.

The solution-focused approach of accepting that people are able to solve problems and find solutions is not just wishful thinking; it is backed up by research that shows that implicit knowledge plays an important part in being successful in all sorts of fields. Studies also show that focusing on an optimistic solution-focused approach can enhance performance.

WHAT DOES THE RESEARCH SHOW?

Studies in the USA on salespeople and their outlook on life showed that those with a more optimistic outlook performed better. The report recommends that management devote time and energy to developing the optimism of new recruits to sales teams.

Optimism and street-smarts: Identifying and improving salesperson intelligence.

Journal of Personal Selling and Sales Management, 1999, **19**(3): 17–33, Pi Sigma Epsilon, USA

Solution-focused coaching works from each individual's perspective. The solution-focused approach is not really new. It may not have had a name before but it is the way successful people have always worked.

The subject who wishes for a tree to be laid across a stream to enable him to cross it, imagines in fact the problem is already solved . . . he proceeds from the target situation to the given situation . . . through a reversal sequence of operations. Ernst Mach (1838–1916), Austrian physicist and philosopher

Analyzing a problem, trying to sort out all the causes may sometimes be necessary but is very often no help at all in actually solving the problem.

Example

John works for an organization that provides management consultancy and IT services. He is a programme director. He spends a lot of time travelling, visiting clients and partners. His company operates a *hot desk* policy, so although John is attached to an office he has no specific desk within that office. John likes to work from home whenever possible.

John's boss Jim feels John should be in the office unless he is away somewhere on business. He asks John not to work from home. John feels offended and annoyed. Jim feels he is within his rights, as John's line manager, to insist he come into the office. There is bad feeling between them. John grudgingly puts in a bit more time at the office but is resentful and demotivated.

Applying solution-focused principles, do John and Jim need to…

◆ Construct a shared ideal outcome?

◆ Start with the smallest change?

◆ Anchor this down the system?

John decides to ask Jim: '*Do you want me in the office all the time, or do you just want to be able to see me regularly on a face-to-face basis?*'

Jim thinks about it and says:

'*I don't need you in the office all the time. But I don't want to feel like we're not really in touch which is how I feel at the moment.*'

John considers what his boss has says. He realizes that regular visual contact is what Jim is looking for. It feels controlling to John but Jim needs concrete contact.

Having redefined the issue John suggests that they make sure all his meetings are scheduled at a time when Jim is in the office. They also schedule in a regular weekly meeting in the office in addition to phone and email contact. They also agree to re-assess the situation in two weeks' time.

It may be that this dispute over working arrangements is hiding a much deeper conflict or problem (quite probable). If either of them tries to force the issue they are likely to get entrenched in the wrong problem. By making very small adjustments they are more likely to move towards a useful solution.

Solution-focused thinking is not about ignoring problems – it is about reframing them. We do it all the time anyway, but coaching sets out to make this explicit and deliberate.

We are much more used to the problem-focused approach. And sometimes this can be a very necessary way of working.

But even in medical science, a solution may be found almost by chance, before the problem is fully understood. This is the 'Eureka!' moment when seemingly unrelated thoughts or intuitions come together and a new idea or understanding is created.

Insight is typically an 'Aha' phenomenon, not a step-by-step assembly of parts of the solution. Our brains are complex adaptive systems. Not machines. Lewin and Regine.[9]

Scientists report moments of insight when the answer to a problem seems to come out of the blue. Inventor Trevor Baylis was watching a TV programme about the devastation caused by AIDS in Africa. The narrator described how one of the main problems was getting health education to remote villages. Many villages had no mains electricity and batteries were expensive and hard to come by. Solar power wasn't the answer as most people listened to the radio in the evening after dark. Trevor thought about the old wind-up gramophones and how much sound they could produce.

I had this glaring flash of something so obvious a child of six could have thought of it. If a clockwork gramophone can produce that volume of sound, then why not apply the principle to building a spring-driven radio. Trevor Baylis

Solution-focused thinking is not about ignoring problems – it is about reframing them. We do it all the time anyway, but coaching sets out to make this explicit and deliberate.

Many of the most important discoveries are made seemingly by accident. The key lies perhaps in being open and receptive enough to notice new discoveries and ideas when they come along.

Alexander Fleming discovered penicillin by accident. He knew what he was looking for: he wanted something that would kill bacteria. When the blue mould in his petri dish seemed to be clearing a space around itself, he worked backwards from the evidence and discovered that it was penicillin that had done the trick.

Archimedes was taking a bath when he suddenly understood the concept of specific gravity. Legend has it that he leapt out of the water shouting 'Eureka!' (I have it). Working backwards from his experience of the water being displaced, he understood the problem.

The mathematician Gauss had been struggling to prove a theorem for years. Suddenly he understood the solution; it simply came to him.

Finally, two days ago, I succeeded, not on account of painful efforts, but by the grace of God. Like a sudden flash of lightning, the riddle happened to be solved. I myself cannot say what was the conducting thread which connected what I previously knew with what made my success possible. Anthony Storr. *Music and the Mind*

The harder I practise, the luckier I seem to get. Arnold Palmer, golfer

We are not suggesting that all answers can be found, simply by waiting for inspiration. We have to put the groundwork in. Often this means a lot of hard work. The virtuoso musician has spent a life time in practice, the surgeon has studied for years, the master carpenter has hit his thumb many times with the hammer . . . expertise takes practice, effort and time. Then the inspiration comes.

So, we can't just wait for flashes of inspiration and moments of insight. They come along too rarely for most of us. But we can develop a kind of approach and a way of looking at the world that encourages this kind of thinking. We can also accept that solutions do not necessarily build up in a step-by-step, linear fashion but rather gradually emerge from what seems to be chaos.

This emergent quality is all around us. Music uses it. Many pieces of music use recurrent themes, refrains, variations that gradually build to the moment where suddenly everything seems to fall into place and the whole orchestra is playing the main theme in harmony. Then we realize that we have been hearing this melody building up and we can actually see where it was leading all along.

Many pieces of music use recurrent themes, refrains, variations that gradually build to the moment where suddenly everything seems to fall into place and the whole orchestra is playing the main theme in harmony.

If you start looking for solutions, you start to find them. It is like the famous drawing that looks like an old lady if you look at it in one way and a young woman if you look in another way. The picture doesn't change. The only change that takes place is a mental shift inside the head of the observer.

Once you start to see solutions rather than problems it becomes easier. It's as though you start to notice solutions around you. Like when you buy a dog or a new car. Suddenly the world is full of dogs or your model of car.

Tools and techniques

The solution-focused approach supplies us with tools and techniques that enable us to tap into and use the wealth of past experiences, skills, intuition and imagination that we all have, including the following.

Look for exceptions

However bad the problem or situation there must be times when it doesn't occur, or at the very least, when it isn't so bad.

Example

Eric has a bad temper. Under pressure he tends to lash out verbally at those around him. He can't really understand why he is like this. He feels maybe he is too repressed, unhappy at home, worried about money – there are plenty of things that could be causing it. Using the solution-focused approach his coach puts all these 'causes' to one side and asks him when he is least likely to lose his temper. Eric works out that he feels more in control in the mornings, when he is less tired. He also realizes that he is less likely to get stressed when he is away from his own desk. He finds constant interruptions very difficult to cope with and these are more likely to happen when he is easily available.

Doing more of what works

Once you have started to work out when the exceptions to the difficult situations occur, then you can start to try to do more of whatever you are doing that is making the difference.

Eric begins to schedule his more important meetings for the mornings and to try to get the bulk of his important work done early in the day.

He also begins to work from home one day a week and tries to save the kind of work that needs unbroken concentration for that day. He asks people not to call him on that day unless it is absolutely vital.

Do less of what doesn't work

The direct correlation of this is to do less of whatever it is that you seem to be doing when the problem occurs.

> Eric starts coming into the office earlier and going home earlier. He had felt before that he had to stay late, to show that he was a committed and conscientious worker. He starts to try to put the extra effort in at the beginning of the day when he finds he is twice as effective anyway.

The miracle question and constructing possibilities

The solution-focused approach is about constructing possibilities. At one end of the scale we are looking for miracles, at the other end we are looking for mere possibilities.

The miracle question[10] goes something like this:

'Suppose you woke up tomorrow morning and a miracle had occurred while you were asleep and the problems had disappeared and the solution was present. How would you know that the solution had arrived? What would be different? How would you feel? What would you notice first? How would other people know?'

At the other end of the scale we can ask possibility questions. If things were different how would they look.

Example

A woman in her 30s, Erica, works in a large open-plan office. She works in a creative job and she used to enjoy her work, however, over the past year or so she has become increasingly disillusioned and stressed at work. It has got to the point where she dreads work. She decides to see a coach.

The problem-focused approach

Using a traditional career counselling approach a career counsellor may have asked her to fill out personality questionnaires and based on the analysis of the personality or preferred learning style might have suggested other career paths.

The solution-focused approach

Using solution-focused questioning techniques the coach after some time asks the miracle question:

'If you woke up tomorrow morning and you felt really good about going to work, what is the first thing you'd notice?'

To the coach's surprise the client replies:

'As I lie in my bed and open my eyes the first thing I notice is that I have more than three items of clothing on my clothes rack to wear and they are not black or grey.'

It turns out that the client has a poor self-image. She feels she is overweight. Every time she gets up from her desk she feels uncomfortable and that people are looking at her. The miracle question has revealed the deeper situation.

Reframing the problems

Another technique is to reframe the problem. You can look at the situation from a different perspective. For example, walking down the street you see an unshaven man lying against the wall, bleeding and incoherent. You might find it unacceptable and threatening. However, you might then find out that he lived in the building, that he had been up all night nursing his ailing aunt and so had not had time to shave. Tired after spending a night at the hospital he has tripped over and cracked his head on the kerb. You just happen to be the first person to come along – you now see the situation from another point of view. Sometimes taking this different view is a choice that we have.

Reframing changes the meaning we give to a situation.[11] For example, your mother phones you every day because she loves you and wants to talk to you. You might see this as controlling and interfering or you can choose to reframe this as the behaviour of a concerned, elderly mother.

Your team keep asking you questions. They can't seem to get on with anything by themselves. As their manager you are being driven mad. Reframe the problem. They want to do a good job; they want to please you; they want to get it right. This willingness and eagerness to please is something you can use in a positive way. It is not just an irritation.

Reframing is about changing the meaning we give to events, not necessarily changing the events themselves.

Erica has very poor self-image. Because of this she hates and is frightened of going shopping for clothes. She wears drab clothes that she doesn't like and so feels even worse about herself. Together with her coach she works out a way forward. They formulate a plan that will enable Erica to buy herself some clothes that she feels good in.

Scaling

Scaling is a means of subjectively measuring our experiences and can be used in many difference ways. For example, the coach might ask the coachee to rate, on a scale of 1 to 10, how close they are to their goal. The key principle here is to move just one or two points of the scale at a time, rather than go straightaway for a 10. This small steps approach is an intrinsic part of the solution-focused approach. A key problem in change is trying to do too much too soon.[12]

Example

Erica's first task is to identify where she is on the change scale. Her coach asks her to rate her ability to go out and buy new clothes that will make her look and feel good. On a scale of 1 to 10, where 10 represents supreme confidence in buying new clothes, she rates herself as a 4. A 5 represents just looking in the shop window and, for her first homework, this is what she does.

The next task (rated a 6) is to go into the shop and look, but again not buy. Again she has to rate her feelings.

After some time she has gained the confidence to buy herself a new garment.

By setting herself small steps and each time observing her feelings Erica gradually manages to buy and wear clothes that she likes and that make her feel good about herself.

Six months after first seeing the coach she is able to reappraise her situation. She decides that she wants a career break and hands in her notice to set off on a round-the-world trip. She has completely changed her outlook on life.

This technique of scaling not only gives you a completely subjective and personalized tool for examining your own perceptions and views of any situation, it also provides you with a unit of measurement for something that may not be quantifiable in any other way.

Example

Jan plays tennis. He enjoys it and would like to play more but he feels he is not very good. His coach asks him to rate himself on a scale from 1 to 10, where 1 is a very poor player with little natural ability and 10 is an exceptionally good professional standard player. Jan rates himself as a 3.

The coach congratulates him. He is one-third of the way there already! The coach can now get Jan to work out what it is that has got him to a 3. What is he already good at? Then he asks him to work out how he could get to a 4 and how he would know he was there.

Using resources

We often have more resources at our disposal than we realize. By drawing on these resources we can often achieve more than we realize.

Example

Staff at a London comprehensive school find it difficult to provide everything they would like for the children. The playground is run down, the sports pitches are in a bad state. The school has little money for trips and outings.

The PTA and the staff get together to decide what they can do. The usual round of fund-raising events is suggested: Christmas fairs, quiz nights etc. Then one of the parents suggests a skills directory for the parents. They decide to put together a directory of skills that the parents of the children in the school have. They don't have to offer to give any time at this stage, just to say what they can do.

They send a circular email to all the parents in the school asking them to list their skills and whether they would be able to give some time to help the school. They find that they have journalists, photographers, bricklayers, gardeners, a violin maker, a professional chess player, musicians, events organizers, bookkeepers, speakers of 16 different languages, landscape architects, bakers and many other professional, semi-professional and amateur skills.

They decide to use the skills of these parents to enhance the effectiveness of the money they raise by traditional means.

Solution-focused coaching uses techniques to make implicit knowledge, skills and talents explicit.

Example

A manager at a psychiatric hospital was having difficulty with her team. She decided to try some solution-focused techniques to get them thinking positively. She tried a few questions:

Can you recall a time when you felt especially effective as a therapist?
Are there moments when you have felt like a good team player?

What do you consider to be your most successful moments in this department?
When has the team worked well together?

The team immediately began to feel more positive and hopeful about the future. They used their answers as a basis for a new work direction.

Solution-focused principles and techniques help us tap into our inherent, perhaps unconscious thought processes and experiences of situations to help us find the answers we need. They formalize and provide a structure to a process that many successful people use naturally.

This does not mean that causes are not important. In many situations, it is vital to understand as much as possible the sequence of events that lead up to a situation. In medicine, for example, it is very often crucial that the causes of a complaint be understood in order for it to be treated correctly.

It is a medical principle that before a symptom is treated, the cause must be found.
Professor Robert Winston

But very often, causes are only understood after the solution has been found. Investigating the causes, no matter how thoroughly, does not necessarily lead to the answers. In fact, it is often only when we have the answer that we can really understand the problem.

The really important breakthroughs are always unpredictable. It is their very unpredictability that makes them important; they change our world in ways we didn't see coming.
Ian Stewart, *Nature's Numbers*, p 34 (Weidenfeld and Nicholson, 1995)

Very often, causes are only understood after the solution has been found. Investigating the causes, no matter how thoroughly, does not necessarily lead to the answers. In fact, it is often only when we have the answer that we can really understand the problem.

TABLE 2.1 SOLUTION FOCUSED VERSUS PROBLEM FOCUSED THINKING IN THE WORKPLACE

Activity	Problem Focus	Solution Focus
Planning change	Emphasis on diagnosis "Can you tell me about the problem?" Identify all the blocks to change.	Emphasis on desired outcome "How would you like it to be?" Identify progress already made Highlight strengths and resources
Managing people	Sees people as sources of dysfunction Who is the weak link? How can we minimize the risks people represent?	Sees people as functional and sources of solutions Where are the hidden strengths How can we grow our people?
Monitoring Progress	Emphasis on identifying weaknesses & failures "What went wrong last week?" Record and react to undesirables. Look at how far we have to go.	Emphasis on identifying what works and gains made "How did you cope so well last week?" "When it works well, what is different about those times?" Look at how far we have come
Troubleshooting	Emphasis on explaining problems: Uncover the Cause and Effect chain "Is lack of progress a symptom of something deeper?" Who is to blame	Emphasis on improving progress and identifying do-able goals "What else might help?" "Have we identified the right goal?" How do others overcome this? What other ways can it be done?

Adapted from, and used with permission of Michael J Cavanagh

chapter three
from awareness to responsibility to results

To some extent, a management coaching style is an attitude, a way of being and a set of skills. Like anything else coaching improves with practice. The models and techniques outlined in this chapter are useful and powerful ways of developing coaching skills. Eventually a good manager will be able to internalize these models and techniques to such an extent that they become a natural part of the way they work. They became part of his or her implicit knowledge. But to begin with, like anything else, you need to learn how to use them. In essence, coaching is about raising an individual's awareness, getting them to take responsibility, supporting them in designing and implementing actions and thereby getting results.

Coaching moves people from awareness to responsibility into action and on to results.

It's all about change

Coaching is about creating change. But change is often complex. It is very rarely about simply making a decision. Most of us find change uncomfortable and unsettling. For managers who have to implement changes in their organizations this can be a big problem.[1]

One of the biggest hurdles is getting over people's suspicions. Making them see there's something in it for them. So often people think change is just a cloak for redundancy – or a way of getting them to do more work for less money.

Mind you I was the worst offender. There was me lecturing people about change but at the beginning when email first came I refused to use it. I preferred my PA and dictation. I used to offer my computer every time they needed one for training because I hardly knew how to turn it on.

Christine Turner, Deputy Chairman, Board of Housing Association

Discomfort is your friend

Many of us don't like change, yet change is all around us all the time. We may like to think that our comfort zone is a place of stability, safety and inertia but really the comfort zone is a frame of mind. It is the meaning we give to the familiar. Of course, it is comfortable staying with the familiar.

If we keep doing the same things we are likely to get the same result. If we want to improve we are going to have to step into unfamiliar territory. Feelings of discomfort as we begin to implement change are signs that we are moving forward. The comfort zone is not the panic zone.

Many of us don't like change, yet change is all around us all the time. We may like to think that our comfort zone is a place of stability, safety and inertia but really the comfort zone is a frame of mind. It is the meaning we give to the familiar.

Problems cannot be solved at the same level of awareness that created them.

Einstein

It seems that a key success factor in implementing change is being able to sell people a vision: to have a clear view of where you are heading. Then you have to deal with four areas of experience: thoughts, feelings, emotions and environment.

The house of change

The house of change is a metaphor for our whole life experience.

Research has shown that for change to be effective you need to work on restructuring your four separate life domains:[2] your thoughts, your feelings, your behaviour and the situation or environment. It's important to realize that each of the four areas of our experience interacts with the others – the situation impacts on how we behave, which impacts on our thoughts, which affect our feelings and so on.

If we are going to coach people to reach their goals successfully we need to make sure that they work on structuring on all four corners of the house of change. If you leave any part of the house of change unbuilt you risk the chance of it all toppling over or collapsing unexpectedly.

We need to realize that change is difficult for many people and that it is only when they have managed to change each area of the house of change that they will be able fully to incorporate change into their lives (see Figure 3.1).

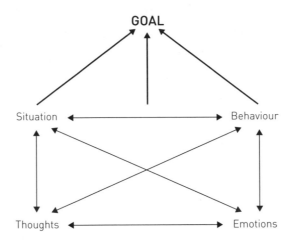

Figure 3.1 The house of change used in an organizational setting

Example

An organization is changing its structure. It is moving from country-based operations to function-based operations. So, instead of the French office, the German office etc., they will now have the sales department, the marketing department and so on, across all the European countries.

This change involves a huge amount of reorganization – and possibly some redundancies.

The manager of the UK division is given the task of introducing this change to her department. To make sure the change goes smoothly she needs to be clear in her own mind the overall goal of the restructuring – create a vision for herself of where the company wants to be. It is crucial that she researches this thoroughly. She needs to understand the overall goal including the reasons behind it if she is to push through the changes.

She then needs to find a way of presenting this to her staff.

For them the new structure might mean:

◆ new premises or working arrangements (situation)

◆ new ways of working – possibly with some training requirements (behaviour)

◆ getting to grips with and understanding the new structure (thoughts)

◆ changing relationships, new colleagues, different feelings about the way they work, the purpose of their work and who they are working with (emotion).

If she is to be successful in bringing about the change, she needs to make sure that she deals with each of these areas and brings about changes in each one. She also needs to know that people will be dealing with all these areas and to be successful she probably needs to make sure that there are some benefits under each category.

As a manager implementing change you need to establish outcomes or goals that deal with each of the four corners of the house of change. You then need to set up a process that allows you and your team to monitor your progress towards these goals.

Beware of the basement

We have all been invited on a social visit to someone's house for the first time. It would be unthinkable as soon as our host opened the door to start opening the cupboards, looking under the bed and rushing down into the basement to see what is hidden away in the dusty depths. But as we walk through the house it is quite acceptable to have a quick peek through an open door to see what sort of wallpaper they have in the bedroom.

Of course, if, as you enter the house, you ask the host for permission to look around, they are nearly always more than delighted to show you around, even though the bedrooms might be a mess.

Just as you would never rush into the basement of somebody's house without first asking permission, the manager coach should never go into the basement of the house of change without asking the permission of the employee.

It is ok briefly to discuss the employee's fears or anxieties about a change situation but you should never attempt prolonged and detailed analysis of people's private thoughts and feelings. Any detailed discussion of these thoughts and feelings should only take place with the employee's clear permission.

Laying the foundations for change

There are four factors involved in creating purposeful change.

Discontent with the present

If we are satisfied with what we have, why bother changing? We need a desire to change; managers may have to work with their people to raise their discontent with the present. But if all we have is discontent then we will get depressed and feel hopeless and helpless. We need a vision of how it could be.

Vision of the future

If we're uninspired by our vision of the future, we're unlikely to put the effort in to create change. But, paradoxically, if the vision we have is too rigid and specific it will not allow us the necessary flexibility in the enactment of our action plans. We need both a broad fuzzy vision to guide us and specific goals to work towards along the way. Manager coaches may need to work with their people to help them design the vision set goals and develop action plans.

Skills to reach our goal

Here 'skills' means both *skills* and *knowledge*. Without both of these we will have the desire and vision to change, but will not know how to do it. The role of the manager coach may be more to act as a trainer than a coach, to make sure that people have the skills and knowledge they need.

Continuous and deliberate action towards our goals

Creating purposeful directed change requires *continuous and deliberate* action – not just wishful thinking. Here the role of the manager coach is to manage the process of performance enhancement over time and to hold the individual accountable for the action plans that he or she agrees to. The manager coach and the individual need to be able to monitor and evaluate the process over time (see Figure 3.2).

In order to achieve our goals, in addition to the foundations, we need to have a roadmap of change. All coaching is about enhancing self-regulation, i.e. the ability to set the goal, to work systematically towards that goal and responding appropriately to feedback, making the necessary changes as we go.

In order to achieve our goals, in addition to the foundations, we need to have a roadmap of change. All coaching is about enhancing self-regulation, i.e. the ability to set the goal, to work systematically towards that goal and responding appropriately to feedback,[3] making the necessary changes as we go. Manager coaches need to help individuals to set a goal, develop an action plan, act, monitor and evaluate change – what's not working, doing more of what works. It really is an elegantly simple model (see Figure 3.3). The power lies in its simplicity. And the role of the manager coach is to help the individual work through this process.

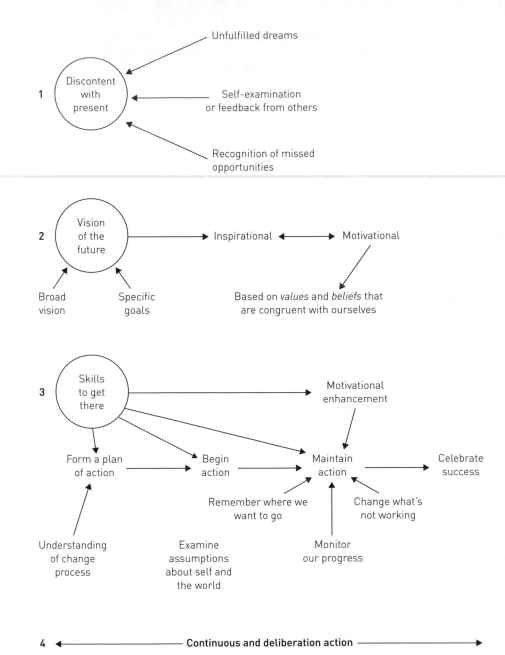

1 Discontent with present
- Unfulfilled dreams
- Self-examination or feedback from others
- Recognition of missed opportunities

2 Vision of the future → Inspirational ↔ Motivational
- Broad vision
- Specific goals
- Based on *values* and *beliefs* that are congruent with ourselves

3 Skills to get there → Motivational enhancement

Form a plan of action → Begin action → Maintain action → Celebrate success

- Understanding of change process
- Examine assumptions about self and the world
- Remember where we want to go
- Monitor our progress
- Change what's not working

4 ← Continuous and deliberation action →

Figure 3.2 The roadmap of change

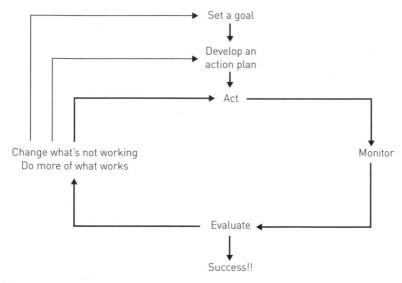

Figure 3.3 The road to success

Fuzzy vision

The first thing that we need to do is to develop a fuzzy vision.

Fuzzy visions and goals

Research shows that goals are vital in bringing about positive change.[4] For goals to be useful they need to be specific, otherwise it is difficult to measure whether or not we are achieving them. But we first need to create a fuzzy vision. If we are too fixated on the end point then we lose energy for the journey.

Fuzzy vision is not the same as a goal. Fuzzy vision is an approximation of the way you want to feel, the place you want to be in. It is not precise and defined. It is a sense of how you want things to be rather than a precise outcome (see Figure 3.4).

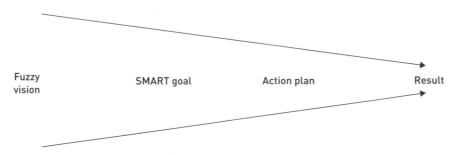

Figure 3.4 How fuzzy becomes focused

Fuzzy vision   SMART goal   Action plan   Result

The skill of coaching is taking someone from the fuzzy vision and getting them to develop specific goals, designing an action plan and supporting them in getting their result.

Coaching can be seen as a process of continually refining the vision, making it more and more tangible until the results materialize in our lives. In a sense it is a kind of interpersonal and interactive alchemy.

Solution-focused techniques are perfect for creating fuzzy vision. In creating fuzzy vision the manager coach simply asks possibility questions such as how would you *like* it to be or the miracle question.

Once you have a sense of your fuzzy vision you need to move on to develop your smart goals. And from those smart goals develop an action plan. Through refinement the goals become the action plan (see Table 3.1).

From Table 3.1 we can see that to be the world's number one nation in space technology is a terrific fuzzy vision, but it doesn't tell us how to get there. One way of achieving this aim would be to kill off all other nations and to have a small bi-plane. We would then be the number one nation. But a good specific goal is as Kennedy said: 'To put a man on the moon by the end of the decade.'

Similarly, to be financially secure is a good fuzzy vision but a poor specific goal. You could become financially secure by learning to live on a very low income. A better specific goal is to have your own profitable business within the next two years. However, this specific goal is still not detailed enough to become a coachable action plan.

TABLE 3.1 VISION VS GOALS

Good fuzzy vision but poor specific goal	Good specific goal
To be the world's number one nation in space technology	To put a man on the moon by the end of the decade
To be financially secure	To have my own profitable business within the next two years
I want to feel fit, enjoy an active lifestyle and feel good about my body	To exercise three times a week, eat a balanced diet and regularly take time to centre myself

Coaching can be seen as a process of continually refining the vision, making it more and more tangible until the results materialize in our lives. In a sense it is a kind of interpersonal and interactive alchemy.

What does profitable mean? It would be much better if we could define what profit meant.

The vision of being fit, enjoying an active lifestyle and feeling good about your body is a terrific frame of reference but it doesn't tell us anything about how we are going to get there. However, if our goal is as sophisticated and refined as to exercise three times a week, eat a balanced diet and regularly take time to centre myself, this is almost an action plan in itself. The refinement of vision to action plan is one of the key competencies a coach needs.

Smart goals

If goals are to be effective they need to be **S**pecific, **M**easurable, **A**ttractive, **R**ealistic and **T**ime framed.

Research[5] carried out in the USA with tens of thousands of subjects over the course of 30 years has shown that if we have a goal to aim for we are more likely to be successful.

WHAT DOES THE RESEARCH SHOW?

In 1996 Edwin Locke at the University of Maryland reviewed 30 years' research into the relationship between goal setting and performance on work tasks. Over 40,000 people had taken part in these studies. The participants ranged from children to research scientists. The studies took place in eight different countries, with time spans of between one minute and 24 years, and with laboratory and field studies. These were just some of the findings:

◆ The more difficult the goal the greater the sense of achievement.

◆ The more specific or explicit the goal the more precisely the performance is regulated.

◆ Goals that are both specific and difficult lead to the highest performance.

◆ Commitment to goals is most critical when goals are specific and difficult.

◆ High commitment to goals is attained when:

  – the individual is convinced that the goal is important

  – the individual is convinced that the goal is attainable (or at least that progress can be made towards it).

◆ Goal setting is most effective when there is feedback showing progress in relation to the goal.

- ◆ Goal setting mediates the effect of knowledge of past performance on subsequent performance.

- ◆ Goals stimulate planning.

- ◆ People have more difficulty attaining goals if they:

  - – lack experience or training

  - – are under undue pressure to perform

  - – have high time pressure.

- ◆ Goals affect personality.

- ◆ Goals serve as standards of self-satisfaction.

All these add up to SMART goals.

Research also shows that the more difficult the goal, the more we achieve.

I would advise them [young people] to aim high. To set their sights at a pretty tough target and don't be too worried if you're not successful at first. Just keep persisting and keep improving your standards and ultimately you've got a pretty fair chance at achieving your desired goal.

Sir Edmund Hillary

For goals to be useful they need to be specific, otherwise it is difficult to measure whether we are achieving them or not. There is a conflict here, however, because if goals are too specific they can become stifling.

Specific but flexible goals

For goals to be useful they need to be specific, otherwise it is difficult to measure whether we are achieving them or not. There is a conflict here, however, because if goals are too specific they can become stifling.[6] If we are too fixated on the end point, we lose energy for the journey. Further, as we make progress towards our goals things often change so we need to be flexible. We need to work through the self-regulation cycle, to monitor and evaluate and change what's not working and if necessary adapt our goals as we move forward towards our vision.

One of the qualities of being human is that we can imagine the future. This is not always to our advantage. Fear of the future and fear of change can often hold us back. Of course, we can imagine what we would really like and strive to get it, but we can also imagine ourselves failing, we can see the humiliation and defeat before us.

To some extent the future is in our control. By setting SMART goals we can work towards achieving the things we want. But however well we plan our lives we cannot totally control all the events that surround us, however much some people would like to try.

What we can do is learn to deal with what happens to us; to apply our life values to every situation we find ourselves in. This is why it is so important to find out what is important to us. To find what it is we are really striving for.

Everything can be taken away from man but one thing – to choose one's own attitude in a given set of circumstances, to choose one's own way. *Viktor Frankl, psychiatrist, Auschwitz survivor*

So, we cannot necessarily choose what happens to us, but we can choose the way in which we view it. However, if you want to change any aspect of your life and feel more fulfilled then you have to work out what it is you want. You can't hit a target that you don't have or reach a goal that doesn't exist.

All change involves ambiguous feelings. There will always be reasons for staying in the comfort zone, for preserving the status quo and leaving things as they are. Except, of course, we can never really leave things as they are. Life is about change. Seasons change, we grow older, friends move away, the company relocates, our skills become outdated. No matter what we do, things change. We feel that by doing nothing we leave things as they are but, of course, this is not true.

No one keeps his enthusiasm automatically. Enthusiasm must be nourished with new actions, new aspirations, new efforts, new vision.   Papyrus

Then again we don't *want* to take responsibility. If we don't make any decisions, don't chose any course of action then nothing can be our fault. The sad thing is that if we never cause anything to happen as well as never failing we can never succeed or at least we can never take the credit for our successes.

So we may not fully or even partially understand motivation but research has shown that there are ways of increasing motivation. In fact, we can create our own motivation. A key of doing this is to set goals.

So what does this mean?

It means that when we set goals we need to be SMART.

Goal-setting strategies – SMART goals

S   SPECIFIC AND STRETCHING

Vague goals lead to vague attempts to achieve them.

Difficult goals lead to greater attainment.

M   MEASURABLE

We need to be able to evaluate our progress.

A ATTRACTIVE

If we don't want it, we're unlikely to put in a sustained effort.

R REALISTIC

We must be capable of achieving the goal.

T TIME FRAMED

We need to have an appropriate time frame in mind.

04

chapter four
models of change

Coaching is about change

Change is one thing, progress is another.

Bertrand Russell (1872–1970), British philosopher, mathematician

For many people and organizations change is difficult. But one of the only things we can be sure of is that change *will* occur. Things cannot remain the same. Coaching is about positive, directed change. The job of the coaching manager is to ensure that change represents progress, both to the individual and the organization. The tricky thing to face if you are a manager and a coach is that the change may have to start with *you*.

I think the requirements of managers are changing. I think we live much more in a change management environment and so the demands on managers are greater now. If you yourself can't change, and I think that's a big problem for lots of people, and embrace change and therefore take the people with you, I think you don't stand a chance.

Joanna Reynolds, MD, TimeLife Europe

In the course of researching this book we talked to many managers from many different walks of life. When we asked them what they thought constituted good management their responses were remarkably similar: good communication, trust, respect and something that came up again *time* and again and that seemed most important, was something like this:

'don't expect people to do something you wouldn't do yourself.'

This was a constant refrain. Many people, from top CEOs to junior office managers said the same thing. They realized that they could only gain respect if they were seen to be prepared to do the same things their staff did.

The real crux of management I think is you have to treat people with respect in terms of what's important to them, but they have to respect you as a manager.

Gary Reason, London Fire Brigade Group Commander Operational Response Division

Change is so often viewed as something to be imposed from above, something other people need to be helped through. This is why, to be a good manager coach, you do need first to look at your own behaviour and at your own attitude to change.

What is change?

There are hundreds, if not thousands, of books, articles and reports written about change in organizations: how to instigate change, how to deal with change, how to lead people through change, how to understand change. There are many theories but none can fully describe what change really *is*. That is a huge philosophical, scientific, spiritual and perhaps even moral question.

How can we promote and nurture change, help people through if we can't even really say what it is?

Models of change

Models of change provide a framework within which to work. They provide a language to use when talking about change. They help us to understand and contextualize change and they provide us with a way of communicating ideas about change. They are tools, they are a way of describing change – and they are very useful to the coach or the manager coach.

Coaching is a conversation but it is not a normal conversation. It is a structured, directed and guided discourse. A manager/coach will not necessarily explicitly use these tools in every instance where they need to bring about change. But if you have a deep understanding of change, including clear and useful ways of talking about it, then you can work from a position of strength and confidence.

Change is so often viewed as something to be imposed from above, something other people need to be helped through. This is why, to be a good manager coach, you do need first to look at your own behaviour and at your own attitude to change.

How do you use the models?

There is no one 'correct' way of using these models. At one level the coach, or the manager coach, may simply have an awareness and a mental image of these models. This will help him or her to understand and deal with change whether personal or organizational.

The pace of change seems to get faster and faster and innovation is crucial to survival for most companies.

A study of 46 important product innovations suggests that the time taken for competitors to enter the market has fallen from an average of 33 years in 1900 to just three years by 1990. Competition forces companies to invest in innovation. Otherwise they risk falling behind and being driven out of their markets.   *Financial Times*, 5 June 2002

So the vast majority of organizations are faced with a dilemma. A workforce that wants things to remain the same but an organization has to evolve, adapt and innovate continually to survive.

Three models of change

The universe is transformation; our life is what our thoughts make it.   Marcus Aurelius Antoninus (121–180), *Meditations*, IV.3

A model of change is a way of representing the change process. It is a framework that helps us to understand and work with change.

I would say that no matter how many courses they've been on, or theories they've read about, most managers just sort of manage the way they've been brought up. They do things the way they are used to doing them. In my experience most people find it pretty hard to change the way they do things. That is why you get so many problems of communication and misunderstanding in most organizations.

Lennart Pettersson, Programme Director, Siemens Business Services, London

When waves of change collide, they create counter-currents.

Alvin Toffler, *Business Minds*[1]

Change is difficult to carry out on an individual level and even more difficult to instigate in an organization. A model of change can help us to understand the sort of processes many people go through when confronted with change. By understanding how we deal with change we are better equipped to carry it out, on a personal or an organizational level.

When there's a big change coming up I get the whole team together to brief them about what we want. Then I see them individually. They've got to see benefits coming through for them. I would then put an implementation review loop in place. You don't just change it once. Lots of people think change is a once only thing but it's an on-going process. You've got to keep going back and reassessing what you're doing – whether it's working.

One of the biggest hurdles is getting over people's suspicions. Making them see there's something in it for them. So often people thing change is just a cloak for redundancy – or a way of getting them to do more work for less money

Gary Tufnell, Deputy Chairman, Board of Housing Association

The three models of change that psychologists at the Coaching Psychology Unit at Sydney University have found most useful in understanding change from a coaching perspective are:

◆ Kurt Lewin's 1947 forcefield analysis

◆ Bridges' 1986 transition model of change

◆ Prochaska and DiClemente's 1982 transtheoretical model of change.

Kurt Lewin is widely regarded as the founder of social psychology. He believed that human behaviour is related not only to personal characteristics, but also to the environment one finds oneself in. This may seem obvious today but was against the grain of most psychological thinking of the time, that regarded human motives to be largely created by urges from within.

The aspect of Lewin's theory that is most useful for coaching is his forcefield analysis, developed in 1947.

The basic assumption of this model is that:

◆ Social situations, and organizations, prefer to be in a state of equilibrium. You can draw parallels with science here – a body at rest when all forces acting on it are equal, entropy.

◆ Change is only possible when driving forces (e.g. new personnel, changing markets, new technology) increase or restraining forces (e.g. individuals' fear of failure, organizational inertia) decrease. If you can't increase driving forces then try to weaken restraining forces.

◆ Once the equilibrium of driving and restraining forces is disturbed change occurs.

◆ Change is followed by a return to the status quo.

What does this mean?

◆ Management of change first requires an unfreezing of the balanced set of forces.

◆ Change is then free to occur either by an increase in driving forces or a decrease of restraining forces.

◆ The next stage is refreezing. This is necessary to ensure no return to the old status quo.

A diagnostic tool

To use Lewin's model you need to:

◆ list forces

◆ break down complex situations into component parts

◆ use visual representations

◆ keep action plans simple

◆ seek to refreeze, to institutionalize the new situation.

This model represents a rather mechanical view of change. It can be useful in a situation where the issues seem confused or unclear in that it enables the manager to map out what seems to be going on. It can be a very useful exercise simply to map out what is going on.

Not much empirical research has been undertaken on the use of this model but it is quite widely used in organizations.

Example

A small environmental charity has been previously restrained by lack of funding but has suddenly been awarded a huge amount of money from central government. They have not found ways to use the money because they are so used to working on a shoestring and do not have systems in place to plan large budgets. This is an unusual kind of change. But unless they do some clear thinking and planning the money is not going to be used effectively. Lewin's model is a useful one to use here because there is a great danger of this organization slipping back to its old ways of doing things. If they don't use the money effectively after two years they will lose it. The manager coach needs to work with the team of the organization to establish overall aims of the team and then to develop some clear goals.

This organization is having to face up to the fact that its biggest problem may not have been lack of funding, as was previously believed, but actually lack of direction and poor communication.

The inner game

Lewin's model is a way of observing what is happening. This fits in with Timothy Gallwey's 'inner game' approach. Gallwey states quite clearly that much of his work can be boiled down to a single sentence.

I have found a better way to change.   Timothy Gallwey, *The Inner Game of Work*[2]

Gallwey believes that change begins with awareness. And by awareness he means 'knowing the present situation with clarity'.

Once you understand the present situation you can begin to change it. Gallwey even claims that simply becoming aware of a situation creates change. He cites the example of a sales-team that were doing rather badly. Their manager decided to try an experiment and so suspended all their quotas for three months. During this time they were to continue selling but they had no particular targets to reach. Instead, they were to rate their enjoyment of their job.

Over the next few weeks they met regularly to discuss how they were getting on, which aspects of the job they enjoyed, which they disliked and how they could improve their overall work satisfaction.

Gallwey claims that by the end of the three months not only did the sales-team have a much greater insight into their work and the way they carried it out, they had also, to their great surprise, increased their sales figures by a considerable amount. The conclusion they came to was that they were more relaxed and open with the customers which resulted in better communication and so better sales.

Lewin's model seems to work partly on this level of increasing awareness. To even draw up the model you need to look carefully at what is happening, to really analyze and understand the situation. Sometimes that is all that is needed to start the change process.

William Bridges' transitions model of change

This draws a distinction between change and transition.[3] Change is a discrete event – where one thing stops and another starts – whereas transition is a process – a gradual, psychological reorientation. Change is an external event, transition is the psychological or emotional experience of change. Bridges suggests that understanding the difference between change and transition may help to create a framework for understanding our response to change.

You lose your job or are promoted to a new job: the event is the leaving or the starting of the new job. The transition is from being someone who is employed to being someone who is no longer employed, or from someone who holds a junior position to someone who holds a senior position.

The transitional model of change acknowledges that all change, even change from bad to good, a promotion, giving up a bad habit, starts with an ending. With change, any kind of change, you are losing something. If, as a manager, you understand this you can help the people you work with to deal with feelings of loss or sadness that accompany most endings. Often just to acknowledge the feelings is enough.

Change is a discrete event – where one thing stops and another starts – whereas transition is a process – a gradual, psychological reorientation. Change is an external event, transition is the psychological or emotional experience of change.

Example

We are after transformation as opposed to incremental change. That's what we're after as a group definitely looking to run up the seesaw and flip the thing over and look back and say 'oh when did it change?'.

Ian Hughes, London Fire Brigade (Divisional Commander, Community Fire Safety)

The London Fire Service is going through major changes. They recently brought in a new system of 'borough working' to replace the old system of central control. Each London borough is now a semi-autonomous unit working alongside other local services such as the health service and the borough council. With this reorganization came two major changes:

◆ They revised their recruitment policies to try to ensure that the fire fighters reflected the community they served. This meant recruiting more women and ethnic minorities into the service than had previously been the case.

◆ They wanted to change the emphasis from being primarily an operations-driven service – just there to put out fires – to being an organization that helps ensure that fires do not start in the first place.

The change required was not only within the service but also the public perception of what they do.

Ian Hughes was Borough Commander in charge of Camden Fire Service – a pilot scheme for the new way of working:

I think if you asked anybody what do you want from the fire service you'll get the answer – I want a couple of fire engines with some people who can rescue them if that's what's required and if necessary go and put their fire out. The question never arises in the mind of the people at the fire service in the minds of the public – What about not having the fire in the first place? We have to get people to see that prevention is better than cure. And if you can't prevent the fire, because accidents always happen, have a detection system and know what to do and then of course we'll send the operational response to deal with it.

Ian found that many fire fighters were resistant to and wary of the new changes, especially as part of their new role was to go out and communicate a fire safety message to the public.

Fire fighters have been selected and conditioned to thinking that the fire fighting, the operational response, is more important. That is their core function. It's that hero thing. They think 'I joined to squirt water to fight fires. I didn't join to go out there and communicate with the public.' We are asking them to do something that many of them may not be very good at that they weren't recruited to do. Their communication skills might not be so great but we're asking them to go and do it.

In this case the fire fighters are having to give up part of their self-image. They are being asked to give up the very thing that may have prompted them to join the fire service in the first place, the image of themselves as heroes helping people in need. They may even feel devalued, that the contribution they see themselves as making has been denigrated. It is important to understand that although the changes may have been implemented quite quickly, the transition will take much longer.

Bridges sees transition as a three-phase process (see Figure 4.1).

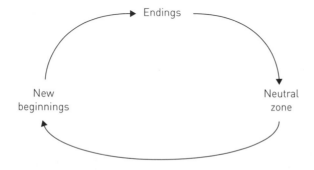

Figure 4.1 Bridges' (1986) transition model of change

Endings

The first phase is 'ending'. In the case of the fire service the reorganization into separate boroughs may represent the ending. This was the most concrete change the fire fighters had had to go through.

The endings phase is characterized by certain things:

◆ stable order becomes fluid

◆ begin process of disengagement

◆ letting go of the familiar

◆ may be grieving and/or a sense of loss.

Neutral zone

In this phase there may be some degree of confusion. The new status quo has not really been established but the old one no longer holds good. Possibly many of the fire fighters were in this neutral zone when Ian decided to visit each station and explain the changes that the fire service were putting in place:

I thought the change needed to be signalled. I had four fire stations and a fire safety office and I felt it was necessary to go and visit each of those stations. There were four watches per station so there's 17 groups of people all with their own ideas and perspectives on what this change meant for them.

The neutral zone is characterized by:

◆ confusion – it is an in-between state

◆ Disorientation

◆ waiting – in limbo

◆ old rules may not count – old ways may not work.

New beginnings

This is when the new order starts. This phase may be characterized by:

◆ risk and uncertainty

◆ possibility of failing

◆ excitement

◆ anticipation.

The fire fighters may, as Ian says, find the new way of working threatening and uncomfortable. They are being asked to do something new, something they may not be particularly good at or sure about.

Bridges' model is particularly useful in understanding changes that prompt a lot of emotion. It is a reminder that all change involves some degree of loss, even change that seems to be for the better.

All change involves some degree of loss, even change that seems to be for the better.

The stages of change model

This is the most researched and the most scientifically validated model. It is perhaps also the most useful. Developed by psychologists James Prochaska and Carlo DiClemente this model represents change as a process with distinct stages (see Figure 4.2).

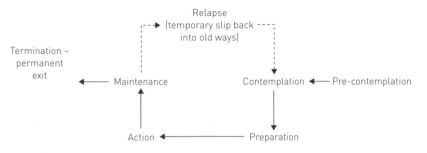

Figure 4.2 The stages of change model

The model can be represented as a diagram in which our actions are seen as part of a continuous loop:

♦ We enter the model from the right-hand side when we start to think about change. This is the *contemplation* stage. The main feeling we will experience here is ambivalence. We want things to change but at the same time we want them to stay the same.

♦ If, despite our reservations, we continue to think about change, we will probably enter the *preparation* stage. At this point we have made the decision to change whatever it is we are fed up with although we still feel quite uncertain and unsure if it is really what we want.

♦ After preparation comes *action* when we actually start to take some steps towards change.

♦ Then we enter the *maintenance* stage.

♦ If we are successful in changing our behaviour we *exit* the model on the left-hand side and the new behaviours have become a part of our personality and our daily life.

♦ *Relapse* is where you end up (once again) doing the very thing you've been trying so hard to change. The key point about relapse is that it is a *normal part of change.*

As people move through these stages their perception of the positive and negative aspects of change shift. As they move from contemplation into action, they see more of the positive aspects of change and fewer of the negative.[4]

This decisional balance is a very powerful psychological process and the manager coach can use this to help coachees in making changes.

Of course, we will probably feel some ambivalence throughout the whole process. There will always be some reasons for staying where we are. Leaving the comfort zone is always difficult even if the change is for the better.

This model could also be useful in the fire service example. The fire fighters will probably feel ambiguous about the change they are being asked to go through. Ian talks about flipping the seesaw but it might be important to remember that. The existing fire fighters are desperately trying to stay in their comfort zone and keep the seesaw in balance. If management pushes down too hard on one end of the seesaw they are all going to run up the other end to try to balance the thing out.

Don't scoff at the anxiety attached to change. The prominent existential psychologist James Bugental called the fear of changing 'a fate worse than death'. Change threatens our very identity and asks us to relinquish our way of being. However healthy change may be it threatens our security, and sometimes even self-defeating security feels better than none.

Prochaska et al., *Changing for Good*, p. 111

WHAT DOES THE RESEARCH SHOW?

A group of psychologists[5] in the USA carried out a research programme on 12 problem behaviours including smoking, lack of exercise, eating a high-fat diet and use of illegal drugs. Their studies showed that the pattern of change was the same across all 12 behaviours and that subjects did seem to go through the stages of change we described earlier. The pattern of weighing up costs and benefits was consistent across the group with the benefits increasing and the costs decreasing as subjects moved from pre-contemplation, to contemplation, decision, action and maintenance.

Dealing with 'difficult' people

One of the key mistakes that coaches make is to treat coachees as if they are in action, when they are, in fact, in preparation. Often just setting a goal with people in contemplation is enough to scare them off or make them appear to be difficult.

Sometimes people who seem to be behaving in a difficult fashion are simply at the wrong stage of change according to their feelings. It is easy to treat everyone as if they were in the action stage, i.e. ready to make changes. Sometimes people need more time to contemplate before they can move on. If you directly confront resistance in someone who is reluctant to move, you may simply push them into an entrenched position. However, you may not have time simply to wait around for people to move on. There are ways of moving them forward.

If you directly confront resistance in someone who is reluctant to move, you may simply push them into an entrenched position. However, you may not have time simply to wait around for people to move on. There are ways of moving them forward.

The pre-contemplation stage

This can be the trickiest stage in that at this point people do not see the need for change or have not even considered changing.

The general principle here is to raise awareness of the changes. The 'better' question is helpful here. Questions such as: *In what way would this change make things better for you?*

You might also need to look at the consequences of not making changes: *You better change or else.*

The contemplation stage

When you want to move people out of this stage you can do a number of things. Double-sided reflection is useful and powerful here. The coach can reflect back the coachee's ambivalence:

So on the one hand you feel that making these changes will be helpful, but on the other hand you're concerned that this will not work out.

- Roll with the resistance – don't confront it.

- Emphasize their individual choice (if it exists): *So I don't know if you'll decide to go ahead with this – it's up to you.*

- Amplify or exaggerate their perceptions: *You feel it will be a total disaster if we implement the new strategy?*

  You think we'll never be able to work with those people?

The aim is to increase awareness but not to push them too hard. You need to get them to move into the next stage. But the harder you push the less likely it is to happen.

Preparation and action stages

At these stages your main aims are to raise awareness of the need for change, help to plan actions and then monitor the changes as they take place.

Specifically, you could:

- Work with the team or individual to set goals – make sure they set the goals themselves.

- Develop a range of options for achieving the goals but make sure they are SMART (see pages 61–2).

- Establish the skills, information and resources you need to reach the goals.

- Develop and agree on an action plan.

- Make sure the team / individuals are committed to action. Draw up a written plan that everyone agrees to.

- Once you start working towards the goals make sure you are staying on track. Move towards setting more stretching goals – use GROW (see page 100).

Relapse

Once you have understood that relapse is a normal maybe even necessary part of change it is much easier to deal with. You need to help your team to accept the relapse and move back into action:

◆ Reframe the relapse as a normal part of change process.

◆ Look for past successes and build on those.

◆ Abandon past failed solutions – try something new.

◆ Help the team/individual to understand the change process.

Why use models?

The benefit of using these models is that they provide a framework. They can be especially useful when coaching someone who seems very resistant to change, who seems almost 'uncoachable'. The particular model you use will depend on the individual you are working with and the situation you are dealing with:

◆ Lewin's model provides a slightly mechanical view of change but can be useful where the issues seem confused or unclear.

◆ Bridges' model is useful in dealing with the emotional aspects of change.

◆ The stages of change model is useful where those you are dealing with express a great deal of ambivalence about the change process.

chapter five
the coaching conversation

The coaching continuum

In-house workplace coaching lies on a continuum from the formal structured workplace coaching at one end to the informal, on-the-run workplace coaching at the other – what you might call corridor coaching: the few minutes snatched in the corridor in the midst of a busy project. Within one organization you might find various types of coaching going on from points all along the continuum. An individual manager might use both formal coaching and corridor coaching with his or her team (see Figure 5.1).

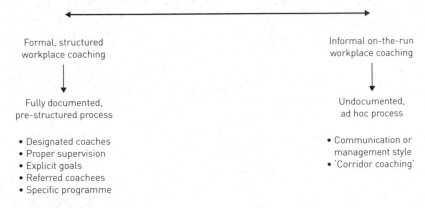

Figure 5.1 Dimensions of in-house workplace coaching

The best place for managers to start is the formal structured end, if only because it is more likely that, from here, things will get done. The other stuff, the corridor coaching, just doesn't happen unless managers are very experienced coaches.

We are currently designing a coaching programme for a group of about 200 lawyers and all the partners are going through the University of Sydney's course. It is going to require a lot of reinforcement and follow -up in terms of monitoring and keeping it at the top of minds and some aids to try and make this as easy as possible for people to remember to do it and so on. I think it will take probably six months until people start to do it on a regular basis and I think a couple of years before they do it tolerably well.   Keith Steele, Freehills (corporate lawyers)

An organization that puts in place a formal coaching structure is likely to find that the corridor coaching will happen as well. When managers get used to coaching it quickly becomes part of the way they do things.

A formal structured process gives consistency and quality across the organization.

In this kind of set-up you need to decide who is going to coach, who is going to be coached, when and how often. To work properly, the manager coach working in this formal structured way needs to work with people to set explicit goals. And he or she needs to make sure a system is in place to make sure the overall programme is carried out properly.

Manager coaches need ongoing supervision in the form either of more experienced in-house mentor coaches or even outside professional coaches.

Tony's (Grant) course was useful because it had a practical application to the sort of things we are trying to achieve here. We think that if we can implement coaching throughout the org. it will allow us to do a number of things. One, it will assist a leveraging model because there are real constraints on leverage using supervision model because it's very heavy work supervising people who are relying on them to tell them constantly what to do rather than working it out for themselves. So they are less self-reliant. Secondly, we think it's something which will reduce the struggle rate and possibly the failure rate of people's careers not being developed and enhanced as much as they might and that will affect things like retention.

An organization that puts in place a formal coaching structure is likely to find that the corridor coaching will happen as well. When managers get used to coaching it quickly becomes part of the way they do things.

The coach as guide

A good manager needs to open up, break down the barriers rather than saying just do as you're told, which I think is abdication – to say look – we clearly have to achieve something – you help me to understand – tell me when you need me to unblock something.

Ian Coster, Siemens Business Services

As a manager coach you are more guide than leader. Your job, as manager coach, is to help those working with you to identify where they are starting from, where they are headed, the route they might choose, alternatives, possible setbacks and how they might deal with them. You need to help them to:

◆ set realistic goals and long-term aims

◆ explore the current situation

◆ identify options for achieving goals and long-term aims

◆ commit to a timed action plan.

A successful journey requires you to know where you are starting from, where you aim to finish, the selected route and any alternatives, and how the environment may change during the journey. The guide needs to be familiar with the many different kinds of journey people may make and the common setbacks likely to be encountered while on the road. If people keep on failing to reach their goals or destination, there is usually a personal blockage of some kind. Coaching can work to overcome and remove these blocks.

The coaching process itself needs to be flexible to take account of the changing needs and priorities of the individual or team. A good coach must believe in the potential of the people he or she is working with. The assumption is always that those receiving the coaching are the real experts about themselves and their work. A coaching attitude can be as important as the precise procedures and skills you use. Some of the core principles of solution-focused coaching are:

◆ People know more than they think they know.

◆ Every person has resources for improving performance.

◆ Useful questions are worth more than commands.

◆ Each person is responsible for their own contribution to the company.

◆ Every setback represents a learning opportunity.

◆ Challenging (but achievable) goals bring out the best in people.

◆ Very often small changes have large effects. Try the smallest change first.

As a manager coach you are more guide than leader. Your job, as manager coach, is to help those working with you to identify where they are starting from, where they are headed, the route they might choose, alternatives, possible setbacks and how they might deal with them.

Example

Ms P is team leader of a team of middle managers. One of her team has recently been divorced. He is very needy and wants to talk about his emotional life at great length. Ms P is an empathetic person and a good listener. She finds herself spending many hours listening to her colleague's problems. After a few weeks she begins to feel that he is using her as a sounding board, taking up her time, but not really moving on emotionally. She decides to be a little less available and a little less empathetic. He immediately notices the difference and acts a bit hurt. When he realizes that she is no longer quite as sympathetic he begins to be critical of her work performance. He begins taking issue with all her suggestions and seems to be trying to block her decisions. Ms P is exhausted by all of this and is not sure how much of it is real and how much she is imagining it.

She decides to use some coaching techniques on herself. She wants to do as little as possible as she doesn't want to make the situation any worse.

She decides to spend a week just observing his behaviour, noticing every time he contradicts her or seems to be trying to undermine her – and discreetly make a note of it. After a few days she notices that his attitude begins to change. As she is no longer putting up any kind of resistance he has become confused and has decided to try a different approach.

After two weeks the problem has disappeared. She hasn't had to do anything at all.

If you specify the right goal, one which the person is committed to out of choice, and has not been forced or coerced into, everyone's chances of success are higher. The goal can be challenging and stretching but you must have buy-in. A good coach can help the individual to identify realistic goals and to anticipate obstacles.

On a journey circumstances and the very destination can change. The support of a guide and the ongoing support of a coach is often

valuable to help integrate the new information and modify strategy
and goals

Three types of coaching

Within this continuum we can distinguish three distinct types of
coaching:

◆ skills coaching

◆ performance coaching

◆ development coaching.

Although there is some overlap between these types of coaching,
there are important differences in the way that the coaching takes
place. Skills coaching is normally a highly detailed and specific
conversation. The coach needs almost to get inside the coachee's
mind and to make each detail really explicit to the coachee.
Contrariwise, development coaching is a much broader kind of
coaching. If the coach tries to get into too much detail in
development coaching, they are likely to get overwhelmed.

Skills coaching

Skills coaching deals with precise and definable skills. This type of
coaching might be a fairly short intervention. Perhaps just one or two
sessions. The main aim of this type of coaching is to enhancing
specific skills and knowledge. It involves:

◆ identifying current skills levels and gaps in performance

◆ rehearsing the new skill and giving opportunities to practise

◆ giving feedback on the level of skill attained.

To do this well the coach has to help raise the coachee's awareness of
the fine detail of his/her performance.

Example

Mr X is the manager of an IT department. His technical skills are excellent but he is unsure and nervous about his presentation skills. He finds this part of his job very stressful. Luckily, he has an excellent relationship with his divisional head and can talk through his areas of concern. At the coaching session they agree to send Mr X on a one-day presentation course, followed up by as many opportunities as possible to practise this skill in-house in a more relaxed and less stressful environment. He asks his work colleagues to give him feedback on his performance.

Example

Charlie is a sales rep for a pharmaceutical company. He is sent on a week-long sales training course. His boss Charlotte, the sales manager, knows that for the training to be really effective he needs to do some follow-up coaching. In this case he needs to do quite precise skills coaching. The course was a generic one on sales techniques. Charlotte now has to focus what Charlie has learnt into some very job specific skills. Charlie sells to GPs, consultants and pharmacists. The techniques and skills he needs for each one are very different. Charlotte now needs to work with Charlie on very detailed and specific aspects of his performance; the way he uses his voice, the way he stands, the way he greets people, the way he makes eye contact. She needs to check that his knowledge about what he is selling is sufficiently detailed to understand the type of questions the GPs will ask and why they might ask them. She also needs to give Charlie a chance to practise these skills and get some feedback on how he is doing.

Performance coaching

In contrast to skills coaching, performance coaching is concerned with medium- to long-term performance improvement. In a work setting this could be anywhere between two months to two years. The coach does not need to focus on fine performance details as much as the process by which the coachee will be able to evaluate and monitor their performance over time as they work towards their goals. Typical performance coaching includes:

- specifying performance standards for the job and reviewing past performance

- describing areas of performance that need improvement

- setting goals and developing action plans to improve performance.

It is or should be:

- results oriented

- solution focused

- self-directed.

This type of coaching is best placed after or as part of a formal performance review. The purpose of performance coaching is to cement the required behaviour change and improve performance.

Example

Ms Y is a scientist who has left academia to pursue a career in industry. She works in a very male-dominated industry and finds that she is using a lot of emotional energy at work 'fighting her corner'. In her annual performance review session with her immediate boss she finds that she has a lot of complaints to make about the way the organization works, including political in-fighting and jostling for position. In a coaching session with her manager she acknowledges that the political aspect of her job is something she finds difficult and distasteful. She identifies meetings as a particular source of irritation. Together with her manager she:

- identifies her most successful meetings and the projects they belonged to

- lists the factors that made these meetings successful

◆ plans a course of action that will allow her to keep the number of meetings to a minimum.

She formulates plans:

◆ Mentally set aside emotional energy to deal with the interpersonal issues, including some downtime where she sets time aside to relax and recuperate.

◆ Keep a journal of the types of interaction and/or a particular situation she is finding most draining.

◆ Spend some time developing the relationships that she finds most useful and rewarding.

Development coaching

This is the most sophisticated type of coaching. It takes a broader, more strategic approach. Here the coach is looking for broad themes. You are working with more abstract concepts rather than the specific and detailed information in skills coaching.

This kind of coaching is often about who you are. It asks questions such as: How do I work more effectively with myself and others? How do I overcome my characteristic shortcomings? How do I work effectively with people I don't like or respect?

It often deals with highly personal questions about professional, career or life issues. This kind of coaching is often found in leadership development programmes. Because of its often highly personal nature, it is more likely to be carried out by an outside coach.

Example

A managing director of a large company has been charged with implementing structural change in his organization. He's called in management consultants who have designed a new organizational structure. In order for the managing director successfully to create this organizational change he has to be seen as a leader, someone who can work in alliance with the key people within the organization.

The developmental coaching issue is that the managing director is seen by people in the organization as being overly assertive, even aggressive. But he is not aware of this. As far as he is concerned people are being difficult and obstructive. His response is repeatedly to tell people why they really need to change.

In the coaching conversation, his coach picks up that the MD is doing a lot of telling but very little asking and has been focused on procedures rather than people.

Drawing solution-focused and systems principles the coach asks the MD: 'Who are the key people in the organization who you need to be on the side of change? What are their perspectives on the change programme?'

Through this part of the coaching conversation, the managing director's awareness is raised and he realizes that he has not really talked to the key players about how they see things. His homework is simple: to ask the three key players what the most frustrating part of their work is. In asking this question, the MD starts to develop a whole new kind of relationship, one in which he is seen as someone who is concerned about others' perspectives. What's really interesting is that by asking and listening the MD gets genuine buy-in to change.

Ask, don't tell

Coaching is about asking questions. Many people today find themselves managing specialists whose knowledge far exceeds their own. They can't *tell* them what to do, not least because they don't and can't know. If you manage a complex team of specialists across a range of areas and skills, you cannot possibly even begin to tell people what to do. You have to find a way of moving forward that does not depend on one person holding all the knowledge and coming up with all the answers.

Coaching is about asking questions. Many people today find themselves managing specialists whose knowledge far exceeds their own. They can't *tell* them what to do, not least because they don't and can't know.

Robert runs his own building firm. He is very successful and has work booked in for the next two years. Part of his secret seems to be that he is able to acknowledge and appreciate the specialist knowledge of each of the people who work for him.

Adam is the carpenter. His father was a carpenter and his grandfather and probably his great grandfather. He knows everything there is to know about working with wood. I tell him what I need, we discuss the work project every day. But I don't interfere. I could never hope to have his level of skill and experience.

Robert, builder

The journey from *tell* to *ask* is a very difficult one for many people. It is a journey fraught with anxiety because it can feel like you are losing control. The paradox is that it is only by making this shift that you will gain the control you need if you are to be a successful manager in today's complex organization.

I find that the best way to get people to do things is to get them to realize themselves what they need to do. I know that when you're working with creative people a lot of what they do is instinctive. I have to nurture the whole team – getting the best out of them and keeping them happy at the same time. If I push them too hard I know I won't get good work out of them but at the same time I can't have people who don't pull their weight. It's also about communication and trust. They know I will let

them get on with their jobs and support them through it but I
need something in return.

Lucy Jones, Executive Producer, independent TV production company

Lucy is a very successful producer working for a cutting-edge
company. She knows just how to manage a team of creative people to
get the best out of them. In order to be a successful manager coach
you have to learn to ask people what they need or want to do their
job better, you have to ask them what information they need and you
have to learn to ask them what goals they need to set. This is a very
difficult move to make. The irony is that it is only by making the shift
that you actually gain the commitment you need to make sure the
job gets done properly.

The journey from *tell* to *ask* is a very difficult one for many people. It is a journey fraught with anxiety because it can feel like you are losing control. The paradox is that it is only by making this shift that you will gain the control you need if you are to be a successful manager in today's complex organization.

At the moment we have a supervision paradigm and that tends
to be a bit accident prone because people are essentially
directed or instructed as to what's needed and then people go
off and do it. They do the best they can, they bring it back and
then it gets sort of reviewed and fixed up and people are sent
away to do more or do better or whatever and ultimately the
product is produced. But a lot of the emphasis is on quality
control and risk management to the firm rather than the
development of the individual's ability to produce a product of
quality. So the development of the supervision model I think
happens a bit by osmosis and a bit by accident. What we are
intending to do is to develop the partners to be able to coach
rather than just supervise.

Keith Steele, Freehills (corporate lawyers)

chapter six
tools and techniques

Structuring the session

It is very important to structure the coaching conversation, otherwise it is *just* a conversation, a friendly chat which may lead nowhere. Coaching is essentially a structured, goal-directed conversation which aims to bring about positive purposeful change.

The coaching conversation can vary from a very task-oriented process to a more people-oriented discussion. In practical terms, this represents the difference between a conversation where precise performance targets are set, for example sell 50,000 widgets by 15 May to a conversation that deals with working out ways to handle a difficult colleague, for example work on a deal with Fred without feeling resentful towards him.

One of the most common ways of structuring the coaching conversation is using the GROW model.

The GROW model

Sir John Whitmore[1] is credited with popularizing the GROW model (see Figure 6.1). In essence the GROW model is an adaptation of Gerald Egan's approach to counselling and therapy outlined in his book, *The Skilled Helper*.[2] The GROW model is a non-linear session structure with four sections: goals, reality, options and wrap-up.

Goal

When using GROW, the coaching conversation always starts with goal setting. Even if the coachee is somewhat unsure as to what they want to achieve, the coach asks them to state what they want to get out of the session.

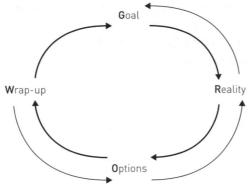

Figure 6.1 The GROW model

The goal is a key foundation for the coaching conversation. If a goal is not set early, coaching conversation tends to wander off track. Goal questions could include:

What do you want to get out of this session?

How would you know that the time had been well spent?

What feeling would you like to have at the end of this session?

What is the most productive thing we could do in the session?

Often the coachee will not be very clear about what they want to get out of the session. If the coachee is unable to describe in detail what they want, then, of course, they are unlikely to get it!

The role of the coach is to help them get clear and define a SMART goal. Having got the coachee to state an initial vague, fuzzy vision or goal, the coach moves into developing clarity about the goal. Doing this involves moving on and discussing the reality of the situation and then revisiting and redefining the goal – a non-linear process.

Reality

The reality section is just that – it's about discussing and detailing what the reality of the situation is. Not what we'd *like* to be happening, but what really *is* happening.

Here the coach has a vital role to play in rising the coachee's awareness, highlighting both strengths and performance shortfalls. The reality section often raises issues which usefully inform a redefining of the original goal.

Reality questions can include:

What has happened since the last session/meeting?

What are the key factors here?

On a scale of 1 to 10, how severe/serious/fabulous is the situation?

What is happening in my life/in the team/in the organization at the moment?

What's working, what's not working?

What needs to change?

Options

Next you need to look at the available options. You may need to brainstorm this bit to make sure that you look beyond the obvious. Here you need to use solution-focused thinking (see Chapter 3).

Ask yourself:

What is the full range of possible actions in this circumstance?

Which is the most attractive to me/us now?

What are the costs and benefits of taking this action?

If you are experiencing a problem with your goals:

Are there times when the problem doesn't occur?

What is different about these times?

How can I/we do more of what works?

How have I/we stopped the problem from being completely overwhelming?

What has worked for me/us in the past?

What can be done to change the situation?

How can I/we move towards the goal?

Who can support me/us in making this change?

What are the costs and benefits of this course of action?

Wrap-up

Before you end the session you need to plan what you are going to do next. So:

◆ List some specific tasks.

◆ List who is going to do what.

◆ List some people who can support you.

◆ What sort of things might stop you being successful?

◆ How will you know if you are being successful?

◆ What will you do if you find these things are getting in the way?

If it's not written down, it's not coaching

Each coaching session *must* finish with a written action plan. The coachee should write this out, *not* the coach. Doing this really increases the coachee's commitment[3] and make goal attainment more likely. If it's not written down, it's not coaching. It's a want-to-be conversation about how things might get better someday when I get around to it!

Each coaching session *must* finish with a written action plan. If it's not written down, it's not coaching.

The I-GROW model

Here the i stands for issues. Sometimes it is useful to spend some time looking at the issues before you start defining SMART goals. The I-GROW model can be useful when the coachee is very problem focused – problem saturated, when they have a driving cathartic need to express emotions or they simply *must* tell their story.

In such cases to push them to set a specific goal may alienate them.[4] The manager coach needs to be responsive to the often unspoken needs of their employees. Good empathic skills are vital in knowing when to push for a goal and when to use the I-GROW model.

The danger in using the I-GROW model is that that you can spend too long looking at the issues and not enough time planning the next stages, so I-GROW has to be used with care and one eye on the clock.

The RE-GROW model

For subsequent follow-up coaching sessions, the RE-GROW model can be useful for the manager coach. The coach should review the coachee's progress and homework and evaluate their progress towards their goals.

Always check to see if the coachee has done their homework. This follow-up evaluation is fundamental and a crucial part of the roadmap of change.[5]

When using RE-GROW, as for the I-GROW, make sure that you spend only a short time on review and evaluate, otherwise the time will pass and no real coaching will get done. Paradoxically, this is more of an issue when the coachee has had big successes. It's easy to fall into a feel-good chat and slap on the back, rather than moving on into a genuinely productive coaching session that will produce results.

These are all good but, they're no CIGAR when the goal is already defined. For performance coaching with pre-set goals, it is useful to use a gap analysis approach. The manager coach needs to help the coachee understand what's happening right now, define where they need to be, examine what is in the gap between and then develop an action plan.

The CIGAR model is far more linear than the GROW model and this is particularly useful where the goal is already defined or there are organizational objectives to reach and the coachee does not have the power or authority to set their own goals:

C current situation
I ideal outcome
G gap between C and I
A action plan
R review

Giving feedback

Feedback is a vital part of good coaching and management.[6]

Good feedback is:

◆ Given at the right time. When the person receiving the feedback is most responsive, i.e. not under pressure, busy or distracted.

◆ Clear and specific – focus on skills and behaviour not personality or attitude.

◆ Constructive – you are providing a service, an opportunity for improvement, not a criticism or reprimand.

◆ Solution focused – emphasize what will make a difference, not just what went wrong.

◆ Interactive – get the recipient's opinions on their own performance. They will often be more critical than you are.

Example

Mr X is a health service manager. As part of his job he has to write a lot of reports. He finds this part of his job quite difficult and time consuming. He does not enjoy writing and is not confident about his abilities; at the same time he finds criticism hard to handle. His immediate boss has to sign off his latest report and add some appendices. She is not at all satisfied with the work but is not sure how to handle X. She decides to do the following:

◆ Think through the purpose of the report.

◆ Look at the report and note down the areas where it best meets its purpose.

◆ Make an appointment to speak to X at the end of the day.

At the meeting she first asks X what he thinks of the report – if there are any areas that he is not happy with.

She is prepared to go through her own criticism but is surprised to realize that X has already identified these points clearly and is quite aware of the problems. He doesn't really have all the information he needs but has tried to hide this fact. This makes his writing unclear and clumsy.

Together they establish that the overall recommendations of the report matter more than the detail in this case and as long as they are up-front about the lack of precise figures there is no real problem.

Taking the small step of first asking what he thought of his own work saved a great deal of tension, worry and bad feeling between them. X was far closer to the work and knew exactly where the problems lay.

A solution-focused attitude, lack of a blame culture and some skilful questioning enabled them to resolve the issues.

People sometimes think that they don't have time to coach. The irony is that good coaching *saves* time. It allows you to focus on the precise situation.

Mr Y is a programme director for an organization that provides IT outsourcing. He is given the task of acting as mentor for a new member of staff., Mr Z. He initially feels burdened by the extra responsibility that he thinks this will entail. But he decides to use some solution-focused coaching techniques to deal with the situation.

In his first meeting with Mr Z instead of presenting him with lots of information about the organization, the department and how they do things, he asks Z if he has any particular concerns or worries.

It turns out that Z is most worried about particular aspects of drawing up contracts and the review process. Y and Z spend time on this aspect of the job and together set targets for Z to reach. They agree to meet once a week to look at Z's progress and review the targets where and when necessary. Because Z is doing most of the talking and Y is doing most of the listening their sessions are totally focused on Z's needs. This makes their sessions very effective. Z explains what he is doing – Y listens. Z gets the help he needs; Y doesn't waste time explaining things that Z either already knows or doesn't need to know.

Y has taken a relatively small step. He has adjusted his management style just a little but the effect is profound. He is now asking not telling.

Coaching is also about careful observation of the situation. Good solution-focused questioning can help to pinpoint specific and precise areas that need attention.

People sometimes think that they don't have time to coach. The irony is that good coaching *saves* time. It allows you to focus on the precise situation.

Coaching is about communication

In order to be a good manager coach you need to be able to communicate clearly and cleanly.[7] You can use specific questioning techniques to draw out feelings, concepts and understanding from the people you are working with.

Asking questions

A prudent question is one-half of wisdom.

Francis Bacon (1561–1626), English philosopher, statesman, essayist

Coaching is essentially a dialogue or conversation. The coaching conversation is about promoting self-discovery and, through this, enabling people to take responsibility for their own actions. It is about establishing trust. It is about asking rather than telling. To be a good coach you need to be able to ask useful and powerful questions.

Why ask questions?

Questions are the basic building blocks of verbal communication. Most questions need some kind of response. They are the beginning of a conversation. Coaching encourages self-discovery.

In many fields of endeavour asking the right question is as important as the answer, if not more so.

In Douglas Adam's science-fiction novel, *The Hitchhiker's Guide to the Galaxy*, the philosophers Majikthise and Vroomfondel ask the computer 'Deep thought' to calculate the answer to the Great Question in Life the Universe and Everything. After seven and a half million years the computer comes back with the answer 42.

'Forty-two!' yelled Loonquawl. 'Is that all you've got to show for seven and a half million years work?'

'I checked it very thoroughly,' said the computer 'and that
quite definitely is the answer. I think the problem to be quite honest
with you, is that you've never actually known what the question is.'

In order to be a good manager coach you need to be able to communicate clearly and cleanly.[7] You can use specific questioning techniques to draw out feelings, concepts and understanding from the people you are working with.

A good coach uses very deliberate questioning techniques that push the client, gently but firmly towards uncovering critical issues, setting goals and forming a workable action plan.

Coaching questions serve many purposes. They can:

◆ stimulate conversation

◆ gain information

◆ develop shared understandings

◆ check agreement

◆ build rapport and trust

◆ help the client reach their goals.

Don't ask why – every why question is better put as a how to

Ironically, although questioning is a vital part of coaching. the question *why* tends not to be a very useful one. Why? is a huge and often unanswerable question. To answer it you have to look backwards.

Asking why questions is a very interesting philosophical endeavour but it is not a useful coaching question. It doesn't necessarily tell us where we want to go.

Example

In 1988 Tony was sitting in a small café on Magnetic Island, just off the Queensland coast. His friend said to him: 'They're doing trips over there on banana boats; let's have a go.' Tony was rather enjoying his breakfast and was not very keen to go but to please his friend and on a whim he said, yes OK. During the boat trip Tony's leg got trapped and his right femur was broken in two places. It was a very serious injury.

There was no point in Tony asking, 'Why did I agree to go?' That was not going to help him get better. He needed to learn how to get up and walk again. The question he needed was: 'How am I going to learn to walk again?' *Why* was not much good to him.

Why is about justifying what's happened and explaining feelings; it doesn't solve problems. This is not to say that why is not important or interesting. It's just that in itself it tends not move us forward.

Frank has poor interpersonal skills. He is shy and awkward in company. He wishes he were like *other people*. As it happens, Frank's father was very overbearing and disapproving when Frank was a child. He believed in the old 'children should be seen and not heard' idea. This may well be why Frank is like he is. But Frank's mother was also very shy – perhaps he has inherited a 'shy gene'. It is an interesting question and may be worth looking into in a spirit of philosophical or psychological enquiry. But asking 'why' Frank is shy is not a very pragmatic approach to the problem. Instead, you should say to Frank: 'If you were feeling comfortable with other people, what would be different?' 'How would you know things were getting better?'

These sorts of practical solution-focused question start to move Frank towards his goal of 'being like other people'. They may help him to appreciate that he already is more comfortable with other people than he realizes.

I took a group of kids to Richmond park. It was amazing. Some of these children have hardly ever been out of the city. One little boy just ran and ran and ran – as though he had never felt that kind of freedom before. When I got back my colleague said to me 'Why did you take them there?' It really annoyed me. I can't say exactly why we went just there, but I do know that every one of those children got a lot out of that trip.

D, learning mentor, Hounslow Manor School

In this case D's colleague may have felt that the trip to the park was not a useful or valuable experience for the children. It may not have fitted in with the programme of study; it may have been inappropriate for many reasons. But *why*? as a question just wasn't helpful here.

He could have asked instead:

What did you hope to get out of the trip?

What did you get out of the trip?

How have you used the experience?

What did the children take away from it?

Was it something you feel we should do again?

There are lots of ways of asking about the trip that would turn it into a useful experience. Why doesn't really do anything. It is too big a question and implies a subtle criticism, even if this is not intended.

Why is about cause and effect. Any parent will know that sometimes maddening stage when a toddler asks endless 'why?' questions. Children often ask 'why?' when they don't know how to formulate any other kind of question. They need more information but the only way they can ask for it is by using why.

Some parents have worked out that one helpful way of dealing with children's 'why' questions is to treat them as 'tell me more about' questions. Because this is often what they want, more information,

Why is about justifying what's happened and explaining feelings; it doesn't solve problems. This is not to say that why is not important or interesting. It's just that in itself it tends not move us forward.

related to the subject. 'Why' is the only way they know how to ask for more detail.

In a coaching context, there are many other questions that are much more useful and informative than why?:

What do you hope to achieve?

How are you going to go about it?

Who will you ask for help?

How will you know if you are succeeding?

These are all much more helpful than 'why'. If you need to look back to past mistakes or difficulties, ue questions such as:

What could we have done differently?

Who could we have asked?

Is there a more efficient way of doing it?

In this way you can focus much more on solutions and outcomes. They are not about apportioning blame or wallowing around in problems.

Open and closed questions

It is useful to divide questions into two categories, open and closed.

Closed questions elicit a brief response:

How old are you?

Did you find it interesting?

What is your favourite colour?

These are all closed questions. They only need a one-word answer. These are good questions if your aim is to:

◆ **gather information:** What colour was it? How old are you? Is this the account file you were talking about?

- **direct the flow of conversation:** Is it useful for you to talk about this now?

- **get feedback:** What I am hearing you saying is that you don't have enough time. Am I right?

They are often easy to answer.

But in some circumstances these questions are not very useful. Listen to an interviewer on the television or radio. If they are any good they will avoid closed questions. Closed questions don't encourage or even allow the person being interviewed to open up and talk. If you listen to a bad interview that doesn't seem to get off the ground it is often because the interviewer is asking too many closed questions.

Open questions cannot be answered with a simple yes/no response. They require a longer, more complex answer and are more stimulating and informative than closed questions. In a coaching context they often begin with:

'What . . . do you think / feel . . . ?'

'How . . . could you . . . ?'

Closed questions don't encourage or even allow the person being interviewed to open up and talk. If you listen to a bad interview that doesn't seem to get off the ground it is often because the interviewer is asking too many closed questions.

A truly open question does not lead the answer. So we ask 'What could we do to improve our sales?', rather than 'In what way would a new training programme improve our sales?'

Open questions:

- **promote self-discovery and empowerment:** How do you think that coaching will work for you? What barriers do you think you would need to overcome to do reach your target?

◆ **can be used to draw out a wide range of responses and options:**
If things were going really well – what would be different . . . ?

In general

Open questions are useful for exploring feelings and options.

Closed questions are useful for gathering facts and directing the conversation.

Asking questions is very empowering not just in the sense that it is effective but it also makes you feel more in control than when you're trying to give solutions. Because you don't start with the proposition that you have to have all the answers and therefore as you're asking these questions starting with a no idea frame of mind. And I was actually coaching someone where I had no knowledge in the area that they were working. But you actually end up feeling quite in control, particularly as they feed you information and you're making connections and you're helping them to develop the options sometimes you can see the options they're going to suggest before they suggest them. The way I felt was 'big shoulders', you know that sense of still having control of the situation even though you started off feeling 'I don't know where this is going. I don't know how I'm going to achieve this'. Kate, lawyer, learning how to be a manager coach

Learning to ask the right questions

Learning to ask the right kind of questions is not the same as learning what to ask about. The subject matter is not the point here, the point is how the question is phrased. Good communication is a skill. Some people are better at it than others but like most skills it can be improved and developed. If you practise asking questions in a way that elicits more information or helps either you or the person you are talking to feel more comfortable, then you will probably find yourself using the techniques more and more. Soon it becomes part of your normal behaviour. It is quite simply a more efficient way of communicating.

Good managers need to know what their team is doing – they have to ask questions, it is part of the job. But they need to ask the right kind of questions, questions that look forwards not backwards and questions that will get them the information they want and need.

Listening

Listening is a key skill in coaching. The coach has to listen 70–80% of the time. This is not as easy as it sounds. People in conversation often do not listen to one another very well. It is very common for people to interrupt one another, give advice, tell each other where they went wrong, pull the conversation round to what they want to talk about.

Deep empathetic listening of the type you need to use when coaching involves listening carefully to tone voice, emotional content, being able to reflect back and tuning in to what the person is saying.

Being able to cope with ambiguity is essential for good listening during the coaching conversation.

Coaching is about change and change almost always involves ambiguous feelings. Change is about loss as well as gain. As a coaching manager you need to understand that ambiguity, both wanting and not wanting things to change are part of the process. If you understand this and don't feel that you have to push the client towards action or a solution before they are ready then you will be better able to listen.

If you are going to ask a series of rigorous and challenging questions, you need to be very aware of when you are reaching the heart of the matter, the action or goal that really will move the individual forward.

Deep empathetic listening of the type you need to use when coaching involves listening carefully to tone voice, emotional content, being able to reflect back and tuning in to what the person is saying.

Clarification

One way that you can indicate that you are listening attentively and that you can be sure that you have really understood and heard what the person is saying is to reframe it and feed it back to them.

Coach: So, what I hear you saying is that you are not clear about what is expected of you at work?

Client: No, the messages seem very confused sometimes.

Coach: What would you need to be more certain of what is required?

Client: I'd like a list of the things we have to do and some idea of the time frame?

Here the coach checks that she has understood what the client is finding difficult and then gets him to articulate what it is he needs.

The stages of change model presented in Chapter 4 outlines the different stages of change. At each stage, ambiguity is an important factor. By making this ambiguity explicit to the client you can help them to work towards a solution. This works for groups as well as individuals.

The seesaw

Most of us want to stay in our comfort zone. We don't want things to change; we want things to remain in balance. It is as if we are trying to keep a seesaw level. If someone comes along and jumps on one end of the seesaw, upsetting the equilibrium, the most natural reaction is to run up to the other end to balance things up again. So the harder you push people in one direction, the more likely they are, on many occasions, to pull as hard as possible in the other direction. All they are doing is trying to keep the seesaw balanced.

Discussion

Coaching is about discussion. It is about helping the people you are working with to deepen their understanding of the situation and options. It is not about persuading people to do things.

Remember:

◆ You want people to find solutions that they fully understand and believe in – don't *give* them the answers. Let them tell you what they need.

◆ Use short response and focused questions.

◆ Give yourself time to think – don't jump in too quickly.

Plan

Talking and listening are important but it is vital that your coaching session is not just a discussion with no outcome. To move things forward you need action. Make sure each coaching session ends with an agreed *written* plan of action.

Use a structure for the coaching session to develop a framework for planning.

Keep it simple and keep it SMART.

Support

For some people it can feel difficult to give praise to those you are working with. People often feel self-conscious or even patronizing when they offer compliments. But by affirming even small movements towards the overall goal you can greatly help your team's motivation for change.

You can provide affirmation when people:

◆ do something that moves them in the desired direction

◆ are able to resist or reduce problematic behaviours.

Reframing and rethinking

Many people hold limited underlying beliefs about themselves or the situations they find themselves in.[8] Reframing and rethinking are core coaching skills. A skilful manager can use these techniques to move people from resistance to cooperation.

Rethinking questions challenges limiting beliefs:

Negative statement	Rethinking response
It's too expensive	How can we achieve the same outcome within budget?
We've tried that already.	What would we need to make it work this time?
I don't want to talk about it with him.	What would need to happen to make you willing to talk?
It will never work.	What would we have to do to make it more likely to work?

Reframing questions create a new outlook:

Negative statement	Reframing response
It's too expensive.	It's great that you're concerned about keeping within budget.
We've tried that already.	So we should be able to avoid those problems this time – what should we do differently now?
I don't want to talk to him about it.	So what would be more useful for you to talk about.
It's been a total disaster.	Yes, we've done well to deal with this problem. Are there any key points we can learn from it?
It will never work.	Yes, you're right it's going to be difficult. We need to concentrate on getting the first bit to work. How do you see it happening?

Reframing and rethinking beliefs underlying these statements

I'm too old to change

Rethinking: What have I learned in the past that will help me meet this challenge?

Reframing: I bring a huge amount of skill and experience to the situation.

I can't write good reports

Rethinking: What do I need to do to improve my writing skills?

Reframing: I've found some aspects of report writing difficult in the past. Which bit do I need to work on getting right and which bits am I good at.

They never listen to me

Rethinking: When do they listen to me? It can't really be never. What is different about the times they do?

Reframing: I am not always as effective as I might be in communicating what I need. But sometimes how can I get my ideas across? How can I transfer those skills to the workplace?

The last time we tried that it didn't work

Rethinking: How could we do things differently this time?

Reframing: Yes, we made some mistakes last time so now we know where is might go wrong.

I can't ask X for help

Rehinking: Who else could help me?

Reframing: He may have valuable knowledge to give me. If I don't ask I'll never know.

Double and triple bind questions

These types of question can also be used effectively in coaching conversations,[9] for instance, 'Would you like to do XXX first or would you rather do YYY?'

Triple bind questions go like this: 'Would you like to do XXX first or would you rather do YYY, or even ZZZ?'

Coaching is not about being a pushover or a soft touch. You might have to work quite hard sometimes to keep people on track. The key is to create clear communication by using simple, direct questions. Used skilfully these types of double or triple bind question can move people forward. You can even make them a bit longer and give people a checklist.

What do you think would work best, some extra training, working with a mentor, setting tighter deadlines? What do you think would work best for *you*?

You can use these kinds of question to present a wide, but limited range of options. You can gently push people into making a decision and taking some action in this way. You may need to be quite sensitive and tuned in to the moment when one of your suggestions hits the spot and connects with the individual's overall aims or style of working.

Coaching is not about being a pushover or a soft touch. You might have to work quite hard sometimes to keep people on track. The key is to create clear communication by using simple, direct questions. Used skilfully these types of double or triple bind question can move people forward.

The manager's toolkit

All the tools and techniques presented in this chapter are part of
your manager coach toolkit. You will not want to use all of them all
of the time. Your skills and experience as a manager and as a coach
will dictate which ones to use when.

have you got what it
takes to be a manager
coach?

Some qualities you'll need

As a manager you have to lead; as a coach you have to encourage and empower. As a manager coach you have to put these two things together. You have to learn how to set goals and plan the way forward. But you also need to make sure that the goals you set are shared goals and that they fit in with the inner needs and values of the people who are working with you.

As a manager you have to lead; as a coach you have to encourage and empower. As a manager coach you have to put these two things together. You have to learn how to set goals and plan the way forward.

The manager can no longer be the one who 'knows' everything; he or she must be someone who can encourage and support the team, allowing each member to work in the best way for them but towards a common or agreed end. A successful organization needs a structure that is at once strong and flexible.

Nowadays you have to be a partner and not a boss.
Peter Drucker, *Business Minds*[1]

Coaching, by its very nature, is a very individualized occupation. Each coaching conversation is different. There is no one *right* way of doing it. The success or otherwise of a coaching relationship depends on the individuals involved and particular situations they find themselves in. It might even be the case that as a manager you are good at coaching people on some issues but not so good on others. However, there are certain skills or attributes that we can identify as essential to a good manager coach. To be a good manager coach you need to:

- be skilled in delivering tangible and valuable outcomes

- instigate and maintain collaborative coaching conversations

- build empathy

- raise awareness

- set SMART goals

- develop workable action plans

- manage process

- hold individuals accountable for their own performance shortfalls.

You may not be good at all these things all the time. Most people will be weaker in some areas and stronger in others.

Qualities of great manager coaches

Intelligence

They can:

- conceptualize and reason from first principles

- see to the heart of an issue

- see the bigger picture.

Emotional intelligence

They are:

- aware of, interested in and able to work with their own and other people's emotions

- flexible

- aware

- able to use emotions to help self and others reach goals.

Business and systems intelligence

They:

- understand how businesses and systems functions

- understand how organizations grow, adapt and change

- understand and can create change in complex adaptive business systems.

In a successful organization everyone is a leader.

Alan Yentob, Director of Drama, Entertainment and Children's Programmes, BBC

Common coaching derailers

One way of identifying what it takes to be a good manager coach is to look at common pitfalls. If you are aware of these you are more likely to be able to avoid them.

Intolerance of ambiguity

In order to be a good manager coach you need to be able to guide people through the unknown and the uncertain. Coaching means you have to be able to deal with ambiguity. Even very experienced coaches often find that during a coaching conversation they don't quite know where they are going. It may be that they don't even know what to ask next. Both the coach and the person being coached may feel very uncertain of where things are leading.

A confident and experienced manager coach will be able to tolerate and go with this uncertainty and ambiguity. This is the point at which you are looking around for a new pathway.

As a manager coach you sometimes need to be comfortable with not knowing quite where you are headed next. If you are not comfortable neither will the person you are coaching be.

This can cause a problem. In your role as manager you may feel you need to be seen to be in control and in charge. The kind of letting go that coaching requires can be very difficult for some people. Often the organizational culture reinforces a 'manager always knows best' attitude.

In your role as manager you may feel you need to be seen to be in control and in charge. The kind of letting go that coaching requires can be very difficult for some people. Often the organizational culture reinforces a 'manager always knows best' attitude.

Example

One of the problems we had with senior managers was that a lot of people were suffering from stress-related illnesses. I think there was quite a high proportion of middle to senior managers who were really struggling with their role.

We had a very hierarchical structure. There was one pinch point in the structure and that was where you come from managing an individual watch and go on to manage a station. So you would step across the divide cause that's the break between going out on fire engines and becoming a senior manager. So there's that identity issue. You're not one of the lads anymore but of course you are bottom of the senior manager structure. So everything gravitates down towards you in terms of 'Oh we'll get them to do that'. 'We'll get that group of officers to do that.' And what they found was that was a point where a lot of the stuff got to that level but they couldn't disseminate it below that because the organization had not invested enough in the people below them and so they didn't have the skills. And a lot of it was cultural. It was seen to be a senior officer's job and so you couldn't give it out, you had to keep it all to yourself; that was *your* power and *your* domain. So that resulted in a lot of protectionism and in people not being able to cope with the workload. And a lot of people were struggling. These people had all done the senior officer management training courses. All very linear-type training. These are the theories, now put them into practice, but, of course, it's not easy when you are being bombarded with a lot of the minutiae of the day to day.

Gary Reason, London Fire Brigade
(Group Commander Operational Response Division)

Paradoxically, when you can acknowledge that you are not the expert, you are actually more in charge. In the case about the fire service, management realized that they needed to equip their managers with better coping strategies and to start to unpack the furiously hierarchical structure that had existed within the service.

Coaching without a clear issue vision or goal

If you haven't named the issues or spent time developing fuzzy vision or setting SMART goals you may well find you are walking round in circles.

This is a fundamental problem with coaching and one of the most common causes of difficulty. You need to spend time thinking about the sort of place you want to get to: how you might feel when you get there, what it might look like, how you would know you had arrived. This is not the same as rigidly following a particular path.

Defining the goal too early

Although you do need to develop fuzzy vision and identify SMART goals, it is also dangerous to define the goal *too early*. Very often the first things you talk about in a coaching session are not the real issues. You may need to explore the goal in some detail before you get to the real heart of the matter. In an extreme case, you might spend 50 minutes out of a one-hour session just defining and refining the goal. In this kind of situation the goal often gets refined down and becomes the action plan itself.

Not being able to hold the silence

In coaching you need to be comfortable with silence. It is often in the silence that the insights come. Inexperienced coaches feel they need to be talking all the time for the session to be of value. When there is silence they rush in with advice.

Playing the expert: giving too much advice

You need to give individuals time to come up with ideas. You need to listen more than talk. You need to learn how to ask not tell.

Rush to closure

Don't try to get to a solution too quickly. You need to take time to get to the right path.

Coaching everybody the same way

Different people need to work in different ways. You need to relate to and work people as individuals. Work from their perspective with their strengths and personality. You may even have to coach different people in different ways at different times and according to the particular area you are working on.

Not being yourself

Authenticity works – in order to work with individuals you have to be who you are.

Over-self-disclosing

It is important not to talk about yourself too much. This can derail the whole process. It is not about you; it is about the person you are coaching. Not all coaches seem to be able to manage or understand this concept.

The sessions were pretty much driven by me. If I didn't focus the discussion it would drift into gossip and stories. He was a good talker and he liked to talk about himself. When he started repeating his stories two and three times I thought, 'Well I think I've gone as far as I can go with him.'

Soraya, Head of Human Resources, Management Consultants, talking about working with a coach

In coaching you need to be comfortable with silence. It is often in the silence that the insights come. Inexperienced coaches feel they need to be talking all the time for the session to be of value. When there is silence they rush in with advice.

Trying to solve the unsolvable

It can happen when you are coaching that after a few minutes you feel increasingly overwhelmed, as though you are going round in ever decreasing circles. It can feel as though you are trying to solve the unsolvable.

At this point you might need to say to the person you are working with something like:

'We are going round and round with this – perhaps we are trying to solve the unsolvable.'

'Shall we work on a smaller part? Or on something different altogether?'

This sort of possibility talk reframes the conversation and invites people to make new choices about how to deal with the issues in hand.

This is a little thing but it can be very powerful. Sometimes when you do this the solution comes very quickly.

Being too problem focused

If you experience this going round and round feeling it may be that you are trying too hard to understand what caused the problem. Again you need to let go – take a 180% shift in your thinking – start to construct solutions rather than deconstruct problems.

Exercise

Living the problem

The aim of this is to experience problem saturation.

Take a real issue in your work or in your life. Only think about the problem and ask yourself questions: Why does it happen? How often does it happen? What are the consequences? Who causes it? Who is affected?

Examine the problem from all sides. For five minutes try to think only about the problem.

Then ask yourself: How do I feel? – overwhelmed confused? Too much to handle? No way forward? It's all so difficult. Is this a feeling you want people to have or is it more useful to have an optimistic feeling? Use this feeling as a benchmark. Use it to notice when people have reached problem saturation.

Making assumptions

This is when the coach assumes the beliefs and ideals that he holds are shared by the person he is coaching.

Example

A coach was working with a senior executive who was dissatisfied with his job. Rather light heartedly he said: 'Oh well, at least it pays the school fees.'

The executive replied that money was not an issue – he had enough not to need to work at all. The issue was job satisfaction. The coach wrongly assumed that making a lot of money was one of the executive's main drivers.

Not sharing intuitions

Once you have become relaxed and competent at coaching, intuitions and feelings can be very powerful. If you don't share them you are closing off possibilities.

You can use phrases such as:

I don't know if this is helpful . . .

Can I share this . . .

I just feel it might be useful to XYZ . . .

Not holding the client accountable

Each coaching session must finish with a written action plan that the person you are working with has written down. If it's not written it's not coaching.

Then you must follow up each session – next time you meet make sure they have done their homework.

Session ending

This works on two levels: you might find yourself rushing to finish off the session. Often when you are coaching crucial issues will come out in the last few minutes of the session. You need to allow space at the end of the session to allow things to come up and to check that they are committed to the homework.

The following skills assessment (Table 7.1) will help you to assess your skills as a manager coach.

TABLE 7.1 MANAGER AS COACH SCALE:
MANAGER/COACH'S VERSION

Indicate the extent to which you agree or disagree with the following statements.

1 = very strongly disagree   2 = strongly disagree   3 = disagree   4 = agree   5 = strongly agree
6 = very strongly agree

All information is confidential

	Very strongly disagree	Strongly disagree	Disagree	Agree	Strongly agree	Very strongly agree
Outcomes of coaching						
My coaching is effective in helping my staff reach their goals	1	2	3	4	5	6
My staff value the time we spend having coaching conversations	1	2	3	4	5	6
My staff's work performance has definitely improved as a result of my coaching	1	2	3	4	5	6

The following statements refer to what happens in the coaching conversation itself – not in general day-to-day workplace activity

	Very strongly disagree	Strongly disagree	Disagree	Agree	Strongly agree	Very strongly agree
Collaboration in coaching						
In coaching conversations I respect and encourage my staff, rather than pressure or compel them	1	2	3	4	5	6
I create a supportive environment in which staff feel safe to discuss their own ideas	1	2	3	4	5	6
When coaching, I ask my staff for their input rather than just tell them what to do	1	2	3	4	5	6

	Very strongly disagree	Strongly disagree	Disagree	Agree	Strongly agree	Very strongly agree
Empathy building						
In coaching conversations I am good at showing that I can see my staff's point of view	1	2	3	4	5	6
When coaching, I acknowledge and show that I understand my staff's feelings	1	2	3	4	5	6
During coaching, I give my staff enough time to express themselves	1	2	3	4	5	6
Raising awareness						
By the end of a coaching conversation my staff have greater clarity about the issues they face	1	2	3	4	5	6
When coaching, I ask questions which help my staff explore options and solutions	1	2	3	4	5	6
In coaching conversations I give regular feedback using specific examples	1	2	3	4	5	6
Goal setting						
The goals we set when coaching are always stretching but attainable	1	2	3	4	5	6
The goals we set during coaching are important to my staff	1	2	3	4	5	6
I always ensure that any goals we set during the coaching conversation are measurable	1	2	3	4	5	6

	Very strongly disagree	Strongly disagree	Disagree	Agree	Strongly agree	Very strongly agree
Action planning						
I am good at helping my staff develop clear, simple and achievable action plans	1	2	3	4	5	6
When coaching, I help my staff focus on achieving success through effective action planning	1	2	3	4	5	6
When coaching, I keep a written record of my staff's action plans	1	2	3	4	5	6
Managing process and accountability						
During coaching, I always ask my staff to report to me on progress towards their goals	1	2	3	4	5	6
When coaching, I address any performance shortfalls directly and promptly	1	2	3	4	5	6
In coaching conversations I always acknowledge and praise my staff's successes	1	2	3	4	5	6

Manager As Coach Scale © Grant and Cavanagh 2003 – reproduced with permission

The following scale (Table 7.2) will help you to judge how effective the people you manage are finding your coaching skills.

TABLE 7.2 MANAGER AS COACH SCALE: STAFF VERSION

Indicate the extent to which you agree or disagree with the following statements.

1 = very strongly disagree 2 = strongly disagree 3 = disagree 4 = agree 5 = strongly agree
6 = very strongly agree

All information is confidential

	Very strongly disagree	Strongly disagree	Disagree	Agree	Strongly agree	Very strongly agree
Outcomes of coaching						
My manager's coaching is effective in helping me reach my goals	1	2	3	4	5	6
I value the time spent in the coaching session	1	2	3	4	5	6
My work performance has improved as a result of my manager's coaching	1	2	3	4	5	6

The following statements refer to what happens in the coaching session itself – not in general day-to-day workplace activity

	Very strongly disagree	Strongly disagree	Disagree	Agree	Strongly agree	Very strongly agree
Collaboration in coaching						
My manager/coach respects and encourages me, rather than pressurizes or bullies	1	2	3	4	5	6
My manager/coach provides a supportive environment in which I feel safe to discuss my shortcomings	1	2	3	4	5	6
My manager/coach sets a broad direction for the coaching session, but encourages significant input from me	1	2	3	4	5	6

	Very strongly disagree	Strongly disagree	Disagree	Agree	Strongly agree	Very strongly agree
Empathy building						
My manager/coach is good at showing that he/she can see my point of view	1	2	3	4	5	6
My manager/coach acknowledges and shows that he/she understands my feelings	1	2	3	4	5	6
My manager/coach gives me plenty of time to express myself before offering suggestions	1	2	3	4	5	6
Raising awareness						
By the end of a coaching session I have greater clarity about the issues I face	1	2	3	4	5	6
My manager/coach asks questions which help me explore the issues	1	2	3	4	5	6
My manager/coach gives me regular feedback using specific examples	1	2	3	4	5	6
Goal setting						
The goals we set in coaching are always stretching but attainable	1	2	3	4	5	6
The goals we set are important to me	1	2	3	4	5	6
My manager/coach always ensures that any goals we set are measurable	1	2	3	4	5	6

	Very strongly disagree	Strongly disagree	Disagree	Agree	Strongly agree	Very strongly agree
Action planning						
My manager/coach is good at helping me develop clear, simple and achievable action plans	1	2	3	4	5	6
My manager/coach helps me focus on achieving success rather than focusing on old problems	1	2	3	4	5	6
My manager/coach keeps a written record of my action plans	1	2	3	4	5	6
Managing process and accountability						
My manager/coach always asks me regularly to measure and report on progress towards my goals	1	2	3	4	5	6
My manager/coach addresses any of my performance shortfalls directly and promptly	1	2	3	4	5	6
My manager/coach acknowledges and praises my successes	1	2	3	4	5	6

Manager as a Coach Scale © Grant and Cavanagh 2003 – reproduced with permission

chapter eight
who should you coach?
and why?

Who you are going to coach is an interesting question. This is true whether your organization employs outside coaches or trains managers to coach. Are you going to focus your attention on *fixing problems* or promoting and encouraging the *stars*? Or is your coaching programme going to include both problems and stars?

In general there are two schools of thought here.

Coaching the problem performers

One approach is to work with the problem people, bring them up to scratch. In fact many managers spend a great deal of time working with the *problems* simply because they have to.

In one case I had a bit of trouble with a senior hand, that's the longest serving member of the team. You can get a sort of hierarchy in the peer group. He was very loud, very funny, centre of attention, great team player, but he tried to use that as an excuse for not doing anything in terms of he'd done it all, been there, seen it. And so the way to get him back into the group without dislodging his status and without making it look like he'd backed down was to value what he could bring to the team to give him personal responsibility, say, look why don't you take charge of this function? Give him even more status but at the same time engage him in the process.

Gary Reason, London Fire Brigade (Group Commander Operational Response Division)

In this case, with this individual, the approach worked but it doesn't always. Then sometimes you have to resort to formal disciplinary procedures.

There are, of course, other people who won't respond to that kind of approach. They will always be the joker and you have to get to the point where you say, look the line is here, I've given you lots of latitude to sort yourself out but if you step across that line then there's formal disciplinary procedures that I can use. I'm not a soft touch.

It's never gone that far with me because I think that's a failure of management. Of course, there are people who are just out to cause trouble but I think they get a reputation and I would expect to be briefed if I was taking on someone like that. I would apply the same approach. I would take them to the line but I'd say, I'm not a soft touch. And then I would go formal with it. Gary Reason, London Fire Brigade (Group Commander Operational Response Division)

There is a point at which a manager needs to know when to stop working with someone, otherwise it's like pouring water into a bucket with a hole in it. When this happens, when people are down that end of the spectrum they need very clear boundaries within a performance management programme and, if necessary, disciplinary proceedings.

There is a point at which a manager needs to know when to stop working with someone, otherwise it's like pouring water into a bucket with a hole in it.

Coaching the stars

Spending too much time with the problem performers is not a good idea. At the other end of the spectrum you have the stars, the people who seem to perform very well. Should you put all your efforts into working with these people?

At first this can seem like a good idea. Working with the stars alone will surely raise the standard of the whole team. In fact, research has shown that sometimes the people who are seen to be stars are holding the rest of the team back.

We all know that stars can be difficult and temperamental people who have a great need to be noticed. Or they may have a need to stand out from the crowd and may have many ego issues that go with that kind of behaviour. Or it may by that the stars are the best technical people because these are the ones who tend to be promoted. Individuals with good communication and people skills may have been undervalued. Their strengths may have been seen as less important. But we are now beginning to see that it is people skills that are often crucial to success (see Figure 8.1)

Figure 8.1 'Problems' vs 'stars'

So it seems that both theories, the one that says fix the problems and the one that says work only with the stars, are flawed.

Work with the bulk of the people

Coaching works best if you work across the middle and upper ranges – the majority of people. This way you are more likely to raise the performance of the whole team significantly. Coaching the 'star' is important, but it should not be done at the expense of the main body of employees.

Most people can perform well given the right training and circumstances. If you operate under a sink or swim mentality you risk losing a lot of people.

Many people end up in a management position who are fantastic at whatever their hands-on role is and it ends up that the only way you can promote is to put them into a management role and sometimes that's totally wrong for them . . . One of my perceptions in business in general is that we don't have many good people managers and that causes huge problems . . . I don't think there are many good natural managers. When you come across somebody who is a natural manager you just cheer. But there aren't many.

Joanna Reynolds, MD, TimeLife Europe

Who should coach?

When an organization teaches its managers to coach as a part of their management style the entire organization can benefit. Employees are more committed. Staff turnover is reduced. There is less conflict between employees and management. There is an increase in self-awareness and overall performance is better. This applies to both individuals and teams.

However, coaching is not a panacea. It will not solve all problems within an organization. There are reasons why managers sometimes do not make good coaches:

◆ They may quite simply not have the skills – in this case training is necessary. It might be useful to employ outside coaches until managers have acquired the necessary skills.

◆ There may be little or no existing organizational support or resources.

◆ People and/or management may be very resistant to coaching. If there is no coaching culture then individual managers may find it very difficult.

Most people can perform well given the right training and circumstances. If you operate under a sink or swim mentality you risk losing a lot of people.

If you are working in a very bureaucratic organization but you want to use the type of coaching techniques described in this book the trick is to start small. Develop a good working relationship with two or three of the people you manage and start to use tools such as the GROW model. Lead by example and try to gradually increase the awareness of this type of working. Coaching works on a very individual level. All the tools and ways of working can be used on the micro level with individual employees and teams.

What type of coaching?

Why in-house coaching?

In-house coaches and managers who have been trained to coach are familiar with the organizational culture and products. They can pass on implicit knowledge and ways of doing things to their teams. An organization that trains and trusts its managers to coach is demonstrating a high degree of confidence in their staff. Manager coaches can work very well at the level of coaching for particular skills and coaching for performance.

Why external coaching?

Training managers to coach may not always be the whole answer. Sometimes it can be useful to use some degree of external coaching. Use of an external coach may mean that staff can be more open about personal shortcomings. They may be much more willing to admit to an impartial observer that certain people or ways of working are difficult for them to cope with.

It is not easy to be entirely open with someone who *holds the purse strings*, as it were. If you are on some sort of performance-related pay scheme you are going to find it much more difficult openly to admit to areas of weakness. If you have a negative attitude to your employer you may well see your manager as partly representative of that. You may also feel that you can trust an outside coach to keep your confidences more than you trust your manager. It is part of an external coach's job description, if you like, to keep things confidential and discrete. It is part of their professional standing.

An external coach is seen not to be so engaged in organizational politics. They have the potential to stand outside all the internal wranglings.

Case study

One of the things that I discussed with my coach was the internal politics. When I joined the organization there was one level between me and the board. After two years another four layers of management had been inserted. And I had actually been promoted.

I think so-called management is one of the curses of big organizations. There are people who really don't have proper jobs and they think, well, how can I make myself useful? I'll block a few things here and there.

So by this time I had a new boss who didn't have a proper job and she saw me as a great threat. One of the things we talked about a lot was how to manage her. It was very helpful.

It was a great shame because there were some extremely talented, intelligent and driven people in the organization but a good 90% of their energy was taken up in jockeying for position and doing the other person down.

If those people were able to devote even 50% of their energy to getting the job done, productivity would go up enormously. But I don't think it was a function of my organization. I think it's a general feature of big organizations and very complex management structures as well.

My coach certainly helped me to deal with those kind of issues.

Malek, head of HR in a pharmaceutical company

An external coach also provides a good sounding board or feedback for senior managers. It may be hard for these people to get feedback elsewhere.

Senior execs are fairly emotional individuals generally because as you go up the pyramid, the lonelier it gets, the harder it gets, the more scrutiny you're under, the more visibility. I think a lot of senior management need a sounding board. A coach provides you with a structure, a framework within which to examine issues.

Nick Ayton, Senior VP, Siemens Business Services

Then there is the question of time. It takes time to train managers to coach and then more time for them to become experienced and skilful. An external coaching programme can be a quicker way of bringing coaching into the organization.

External coaches work well not only at the level of skills and performance, but also at the level of overall personal development. A good external coach is skilled at creating a confidential personal reflective space. They can help people with the overarching aims of career and life plans.

A good external coach is skilled at creating a confidential personal reflective space. They can help people with the overarching aims of career and life plans.

chapter nine

putting it all together –
the manager as coach
game plan

Fluidity and flexibility

The manager coach needs a flexible approach to coaching their employees. During the course of the working day there are many opportunities for the manager to use coaching in informal ways: looking at things from the employee's perspective, asking for the employee's input and suggestions, rather than command-and-control telling. being more flexible about how employees do their work, listening for both the spoken and unspoken.

Not everything that counts can be counted and not everything that can be counted counts.

Sign hanging on the wall of Einstein's office at Princeton

At the same time it is important to remember that although this informal *corridor coaching* is a powerful addition to the manager's leadership style, the most powerful performance enhancement occurs through structured coaching sessions in which the manager sits down with the employee and systematically coaches them.

Coaching is a *soft skill* in that it deals with people. It often works with intangibles, feelings, perceptions, ideas, shared visions.

Coaching is a *soft skill* in that it deals with people. It often works with intangibles, feelings, perceptions, ideas, shared visions. Just because it is a fluid, dynamic and intangible process means you need to make sure that you work within clear structures and guidelines.

But I don't have time to sit and coach

Most managers agree that a sit-down, special time for one-to-one coaching is a great idea – if only there were an extra hour or two in the day and if only they weren't simply so busy:[1] 'Yes, tomorrow I'll start coaching. Let me just get this crisis over with first.'

For many managers, time appears to be a scarce resource. They seem to live in a state of ongoing frantic activity, juggling demands, working from the crisis box of the time management quadrant.

It is dangerously easy just to push coaching techniques to one side or dismiss them as something you are too busy to do.

The problem with my boss is that she is so bad at communicating. She'll say ten things really quickly but she doesn't explain. Or she'll explain only half of what she wants. I'll start on these and she'll rush in and say, 'Why haven't you done the other things on the list? They were much more important.' Everyone in the office is waiting to find out what they have to do but they can't do anything because she is the only one who knows. This just reinforces her position as the only one who can cope. I sometimes think she's afraid that if someone goes off and does things properly then she won't be the crisis manager any more.

If we could just sit down together once a week, even once a month and set some clear objectives, work out what we're doing it would be so much better. Then just five minutes a day would be enough to say, OK, I'll get on with this, this and this, you do that, that and that.

To be fair I don't think she's managed very well either. I think the problem goes through the whole department.

Ruben, broadcasting assistant

The mindset here is that time is scarce, and time spent coaching is a waste of a limited resource. In fact, time is always there. It doesn't run out. But often it is not time that runs out, it is our ability to manage our emotional response to approaching deadlines. What runs out is our ability to manage our emotional responses to approaching deadlines. Yet our ability to manage our emotional responses is the very thing that is most in our control.[2]

Time is always there. It doesn't run out. What runs out is our ability to manage our emotional responses to approaching deadlines. Yet our ability to manage our emotional responses is the very thing that is most in our control.

What often happens is that we get sucked into the vicious cycle of feeling there's too much to do. We believe that there is not enough time to coach others, which ends up with our having to do more work ourselves, because we've not been able to prepare others to take over some of our workload (see Figure 9.1).

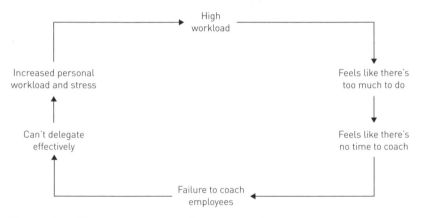

Figure 9.1 The no-time-to-coach vicious cycle

But more often than not this cycle is driven by feelings rather than facts. In the back of our minds are an almost unnoticed anxiety and fear of failure, and sometimes even sheer panic, which cloud our ability to make sound decisions about how we can work more effectively with our employees.

Our negative feelings drive the cycle. We need to stand back and ask ourselves questions like:

How would I like to feel about this?

What am I thinking about?

How are my thoughts driving my emotions?

What is a more useful way to be thinking about this situation?

You need to break the cycle and establish a new way of working. A great place to start is with your beliefs about coaching, delegation and time.

Coaching time is an investment, not an expense

The reality is that coaching time is an investment, not an expense. It is an investment in the relationship between manager and employee.[3] It is an investment in developing employees' business-related skills.[4] It is an investment in human resource development.[5] It is an investment in retaining key staff.[6] It is an investment in improving individual workplace performance.[7] It is an investment in developing effective teams.[8] It is an investment in creating and maintaining organizational change.[9] And, finally it is an investment in reducing the manager's own stress[10] and increasing the manager's ability to delegate.[11]

And the good news is that a sit-down formal coaching programme need not be time consuming. Great coaching can take place in 20 minutes, once the manager and employee have established a coaching relationship.

The good news is that a sit-down formal coaching programme need not be time consuming. Great coaching can take place in 20 minutes, once the manager and employee have established a coaching relationship.

The manager as coach game plan for coaching

This is a very simple, but very effective game plan for solution-focused workplace coaching. If you follow this template you will find that you will be able to run short and effective coaching sessions with your employees.

Laying the foundations . . . preparation, preparation, preparation

Preparation is the foundation of good coaching. Don't rush into a coaching session. You should particularly spend time preparing for the first session.

Remember, you are making an investment. So, choose with care how and where you invest your time. Read, or reread, the relevant sections in this book or other coaching references, familiarize yourself with this game plan, put yourself in the right frame of mind.

There are four main sections to this game plan:

1   assess employee performance

2   the coaching conversation

3   action plan implementation

4   follow-up (see Figure 9.2).

Assess employee's performance – high or low performer?

Before you as a manager even talk to the employee about coaching, you need to spend some time thinking about the person.

Are they a high or low performer? Is this really a coaching session for an average or good employee, or is it a dressed-up discipline session for a low-performing disruptive employee?

It is a temptation to refer to disciplinary low-performance management as coaching. Disciplinary performance management sessions are not pleasant for the manager or the employee. Calling

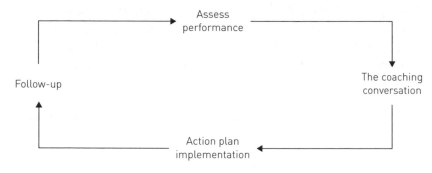

Figure 9.2 The manager as coach coaching cycle

them coaching seems to make it easier. More acceptable. If it is a disciplinary session, then don't call it coaching. Doing so leads to confusion.[12] In these cases you need to hold a performance review and bad news feedback session, and then, once the issues are clear, start coaching.

Ask yourself: are they worth the effort/time?

You are about to make an investment in your employee. Will that investment pay off?

There are many ways of assessing an employee's performance, personality characteristics and their responsiveness to different management styles. These include 360° feedback, personality inventories and psychological measurement. Often these take time, cost money and may be disruptive.

The easiest, most effective and often the most accurate means of assessment is for the manager simply to ask themselves: Is this person worth investing in? Is this worth the effort? It is worth my time? Will this make a difference?

Sit down quietly. Clear your mind and ask yourself these questions. Listen for your intuitive response. Don't let your personal feelings of liking or disliking them cloud your judgement. Listen to your intuition and act on that.

We have found that managers are extremely good at accurately answering these questions. When you've worked with someone even for a short time, you just know. For some managers the key barrier seems to be trusting their intuitive responses enough to feel comfortable in acting on them.

What kind of coaching? Skills, performance or development issue?

What kind of coaching? Is this a skills, performance or a development issue? Different coaching issues demand specific coaching styles. Again, take time to think through these issues. Preparation is the key and makes a real difference.

Skills-focused coaching will generally require a more detailed, specific approach. For a skills coaching session the manager coach may need information about different training courses. You should research this in advance. Or you may need to be focusing on rehearsing specific skills in the coaching session. If so, you should have a clear mental model about what constitutes a good performance.

For a performance-related coaching session, you need to know if the end goal can be set by the employee or whether the end goal is a non-negotiable, organization-set objective. If the end goal is non-negotiable, then you need to be especially flexible in coaching and ensure that the employee has input and ownership of the means by which the designated end goal is attained. Doing so enhances employee commitment to the process and leads to better workplace performance.[13]

For a performance-related coaching session, you need to know if the end goal can be set by the employee or whether the end goal is a non-negotiable, organization-set objective.

For development coaching, where personal issues may be discussed, the manager coach needs to ensure that they ask permission and that the employee genuinely feels comfortable in talking. Here the manager coach needs to be especially empathetic and be able to pick up on the employee's feelings. Because of the power imbalance between manager and employee, the employee may be coerced into revealing personal information. Care, awareness and tact on the manager coach's part is needed.

The coaching conversation

Before the coaching session starts – enrolment in coaching

The enrolment conversation prior to starting coaching is one part of workplace coaching that is often dismissed as not important. In fact, the quality of the enrolment conversation impacts significantly on the success of the whole coaching relationship.

Before you schedule or hold the coaching session, you need to enrol the employee into coaching. The enrolment conversation is about selling coaching to the coachee, enrolling them in a new way of communicating.

You may have decided that it is worth *your* while to coach them but do *they* want to be coached by *you*?

The coaching conversation is different from most everyday workplace conversations. The relationship between a manager coach and the coachee employee is also quite different. Ask yourself, how am I going to 'sell' coaching to the people who I need to coach? What would make it really attractive for them to get involved in coaching?

You probably will to explain exactly what coaching is. That coaching is not therapy or training. It's about performance enhancement; it's not remedial. It's a perk, not a punishment.

Coaching is not therapy or training. It's about performance enhancement; it's not remedial. It's a perk, not a punishment.

You should tell them how coaching sessions are structured and that you will be expecting them to complete simple homework tasks between coaching sessions. You might need to let them know that you will be asking questions that might normally appear a bit pushy.

The right physical space

Where will you run your coaching sessions? The right physical space is important. Quiet. Uninterrupted. Distraction free. Switch off the phones. Turn the computer screen off. If possible come out from behind your desk. Sit at a slight angle, facing each other. If you like to sketch out mindmaps, sit where you both can draw.

Effective coaches use the physical space as a means of providing a physical support which enhances the coaching relationship. If you use a whiteboard for brainstorming, make sure you both can use it with equal ease.

The right mental space – an attitude of service and facilitation

The right mental space is also important. The manager coach needs to hold an attitude of service and facilitation. You are there to service the coaching session and to facilitate the development of the employee. In some respects, this is the antithesis of common management mindsets where the employee is seen to be there to serve the needs of the organization.

Yet this attitude is extremely powerful, just as not being the expert who tells means that the manager coach can tap into the full range of the employee's knowledge, genuinely aiming to serve, paradoxically gives the manager coach more power.

Set the time frame for the session

Time is part of your investment in coaching. At the very beginning of the session, you should make it clear how long the session will run for. The coaching session should be run at a fairly brisk pace. Keep an eye on the time and stick to this time frame. If you start to go over time, mention it and, if appropriate, extend the session. Keeping to a strict time frame is excellent discipline. Going over time can easily become a habit and undermines the value of a coaching session. If you find yourself regularly going over time in coaching sessions you might want to take a look at the way you are running it. What's working? What's not?

Are you spending too long reviewing and evaluating past homework? If so, try using a simple checklist to tick off what's been done without exploring the issues too much.

Are you spending too much time on setting the goal for the session? If so, ask the coachee to think of what they want to get out of the session *before* they come to the session.

Are you spending time trying to persuade the coachee to do something? If so, remind them and yourself that coaching is a collaborative goal-directed conversation. You may need to stop trying to be the expert.

Are you spending too much time getting sidetracked? If so, write the session goal down where you both can see it and refer back to it constantly during the session.

Making written notes during the coaching session

In our experience, writing notes during the session adds considerably to the power for the coaching. If it's not written, it's not coaching.

Writing notes during the coaching session takes some practice. But it is very useful. Writing notes shows the coachee that you are paying attention, that you consider what is happening to be important. It helps you stay on track, too, and saves you writing up notes and keeping records after the session is finished.

Writing also helps the coach manage the large amount of information that is inherent in a coaching session. Coaching is a multilevel, highly complex activity. During a coaching session a good manager coach is working on several levels at once: keeping an eye on the time, focusing on both the spoken and unspoken responses of the coachee, listening in to your own emotional responses and intuitions.

To gain real commitment from the people being coached the manager coach needs to present coaching in a way that is both attractive and inspiring. You need to lay out the boundaries, explain the way you will be working and probably the methods you will use.

During the coaching conversation you need to work together to create a fuzzy vision and some SMART (see pages 61–2) goals. You can then use the GROW models (see pages 100 and 104) and the CIGAR model (see page 105).

You need to develop a written action plan which you revisit and refine at each session.

Action plan implementation

This is the responsibility of each individual who is being coached. It is vital to remember and stick to this. If ensuring the action plan gets carried out becomes the manager's responsibility then the whole object of the coaching session is defeated.

Coaching is not going to work if it means an increase in work for the manager. Good coaching makes the manager's job easier not harder.

Coaching is not going to work if it means an increase in work for the manager. Good coaching makes the manager's job easier not harder.

Remember small steps are the most effective. Don't bang your head against the wall – take the steps instead!

Follow-up

Follow-up is a crucial part of the cycle. If you don't follow up the coaching session then the action usually won't get done. Coaching is an ongoing process. It is not usually a one-off intervention. At the follow-up session the manager needs to:

- ◆ evaluate action plan implementation (using REGROW)

- ◆ change what's not working – do more of what works (focus on solutions).

Finally, it is important to acknowledge and celebrate successes.

chapter ten
why coaching matters

> Happiness is no laughing matter.
>
> Archbiship Whately of Dublin (1787–1863), *Apothegms*

So, why *does* coaching matter?

Throughout most of this book we have looked at coaching from the point of view of organizations and management, efficiency and profit. But it is possible to see the current interest in coaching as the latest stage in the seemingly eternal quest for happiness.

It is possible to see the current interest in coaching as the latest stage in the seemingly eternal quest for happiness.

It is impossible accurately to define what happiness is, not least because it is different things to different people. The fact that it is so difficult to define has not stopped writers, artists, thinkers and philosophers from trying, for almost as long as it is possible to record it.

From Aristotle's 'virtuous activity of the soul' to Charles Schultz's 'warm puppy' happiness does seem to be a central motivating factor in our lives. It is something that we all or certainly most of us want even if we don't know or can't easily say what it is.

The pursuit of happiness may be an age-old occupation but the way we go about it has changed dramatically.

There was a time when the idea that true happiness could be differentiated from religion and spirituality would have been unthinkable. Happiness depended on being close to God. Then, at the beginning of the 20th century, Freud told us that happiness and psychosexual fulfilment were intimately linked. With the rise of the consumer society it seemed for a time, in the western world at least, that we believed if we bought enough *things* we could buy happiness. Some of the things we started buying in the 1970s were self-help books which tried to tell us how to be happy. As one philosopher points out no one else much was asking the big questions about life.

We have to turn to popular self-help manuals to find extensive discussion of questions of the best life, self-fulfillment, the proper role of the emotions, personal friendships and commitments, topics which in the ancient world were always treated in a more intellectual way as part of ethics.

Julia Annas, The Morality of Happiness, p. 10

Now in our postmodern, post-Freudian, post-industrial world we are perhaps beginning to wonder if happiness isn't something we may have to work towards, to create ourselves. It is not just a matter of developing a positive attitude, despite what some of these self-help books would have us believe.

There was a time when the idea that happiness could be as self-indulgent and as ethically and intellectually undemanding as simply choosing to have a positive attitude about your life would have struck sensitive minds as scandalous, if not insane. It is impossible for most of us to conceive now how alien such a thought would have seemed to Aristotle, Cicero or even Thomas Aquinas.

Miles Kingwell, The Pursuit of Happiness: Better Living from Plato to Prozac, p. 77
Random House Inc., New York

Psychologist Mihalyi Csikzentmihalyi has spent more than 20 years studying what it is that people describe as happiness. He found that almost everyone he spoke to, no matter what their profession, social status, class, gender or race, reported that from time to time they experienced a state of being in which they feel strong, in effortless control, at the peak of their abilities. He has called this state *flow*. Athletes sometimes call it being 'in the zone'. It is a feeling of fulfilment, a lack of self-consciousness, almost a lack of awareness of self, a sense of being in harmony, a sense of meaning and purpose.

Contrary to what we usually believe, moments like these, the best moments in our lives, are not the passive, receptive, relaxing times, although such experiences can also be enjoyable if we work hard to attain them. The best moments usually occur when a person's body or mind is stretched to its limits in a voluntary attempt to accomplish something difficult and worthwhile. Optimal experience is therefore something we make happen.

Mihalyi Csikzentmihalyi, *Flow The Psychology of Happiness*, p. 3, Random House, 1998

As human beings we have a tremendous need to make order out of chaos. We need to create meaning and purpose out of our lives if we are to feel fulfilled. We need to create something, a thread, a story out of the enormous complexity of our experience.

As human beings we have a tremendous need to make order out of chaos. We need to create meaning and purpose out of our lives if we are to feel fulfilled. We need to create something, a thread, a story out of the enormous complexity of our experience. This is not new and we all do it in our own way. People who suffer a sudden change such as bereavement, redundancy or divorce sometimes feel that their whole life has lost its meaning. They need to rebuild meaning and purpose into their lives. If they can't do this they are liable to slip into depression and despair. Some people see music and the arts as ways of creating meaning.

Music creates order out of chaos.   Yehudi Menuhin, violinist

The problem for us today is that there are so many options, so many choices to be made all the time. Technology is making our world more complex all the time. As the rate of change increases so the challenge of remaining centred, focused and purposeful becomes greater.

Coaching is about building on potential. It is about working out what you want and then systematically achieving it. It is not a panacea. It is not the whole answer but it can be a useful tool in helping us to choose the life we want to live.

Coaching is about building on potential. It is about working out what you want and then systematically achieving it.

notes

introduction

1   Wood, R., Bandura A. and Bailey, T. Mechanisms governing organizational performance in complex decision-making environments. *Organizational Behavior and Human Decision Processes*. 1990, **46**(2): 181–201.

chapter one

1   Morris, T. W. and Levinson, E. M. Relationship between intelligence and occupational adjustment and functioning: a literature review. *Journal of Counseling and Development*. 1995, **73**(5): 503–14.

2   Berglas, S. The very real dangers of executive coaching. *Harvard Business Review*. 2002, June: 87–92.

3   Barber, J. Coaching: a human capital solution for improving workforce performance. *Behavioral Healthcare Tomorrow*. 2001, **10**(2): SR29.

4   Wells, C. V. and Kipnis, D. Trust, dependency, and control in the contemporary organization. *Journal of Business and Psychology*. 2001, **15**(4): 593–603.

5   Evered, R. D. and Selman, J. C. Coaching and the art of management. *Organizational Dynamics*. 1989, **18**(2): 16–32.

6   Joffe, M. and Glynn, S. Facilitating change and empowering employees. *Journal of Change Management*. 2002, **2**(4): 369–79.

7   Kennedy, S. Organisational change affects work stress and work-family balance. *Australian and New Zealand Journal of Family Therapy*. 2001, **22**(2): 105–6.

8   Hesketh, B. Dilemmas in training for transfer and retention. *Applied Psychology: An International Review*. 1997, **46**(4): 317–86.

9   Olivero, G., Bane, K. D. and Kopelman, R. E. Executive coaching

as a transfer of training tool: effects on productivity in a public agency. *Personnel Management*. 1997, **26**(4): 461–9.

chapter two

1 Erickson, M. H. Special techniques of brief hypnotherapy. *Journal of Clinical and Experimental Hypnosis*. 1954, **2**: 109–29.
2 de Shazer, S. *Words were originally Magic*. 1994. New York: Norton & Co.
3 Osenton, T. and Chang, J. Solution-oriented classroom management: a proactive application with young children. *Journal of Systemic Therapies*. 1999, **18**(2): 65–76.
4 Corcoran, J. and Stephenson, M. The effectiveness of solution-focussed therapy with child behavior problems: a preliminary report. *Families in Society*. 2000, **81**: 468–74.
5 Mason, W. H., Chandler, M. C. and Grasso. B. C. Solution-based techniques applied to addictions: a clinic's experience in shifting paradigms. *Alcoholism Treatment Quarterly*. 1995, **13**(4): 39–49.
6 Quicke, J. and Winter, C. Labelling and learning: an interactionist perspective. *Support for Learning*. 1994, **9**(1): 16–21.
7 Grant, A. M., Franklin, J. and Langford, P. The self-reflection and insight scale: a new measure of private self-consciousness. *Social Behavior and Personality*. 2002, **30**(8): 821–36.
8 Bandura, A., Adams, N. E. and Beyer, J. Cognitive processes mediating behavioral change *Journal of Personality and Social Psychology*. 1977, **35**(3): 125–39.
9 Lewin, R. and Regine, B *Weaving Complexity and Business – Engaging the Soul at Work*. 2001. Texere LLC.
10 de Shazer, S. The imaginary pill technique. *Journal of Strategic and Systemic Therapies*. 1984, **3**(1): 30–4.
11 de Shazer, M. and Lipchik, E. Frames and reframing. *Family Therapy Collections*. 1984, **11**: 88–97.
12 Prochaska, J. O., Norcross, J. C. and DiClemente, C. C. *Changing for Good*. 1994. New York: Avon Books.

chapter three

1 Wright, P. C. and Geroy, G. D. Changing the mindset: the training myth and the need for world-class performance. *The International Journal of Human Resource Management*. 2002, **12**(4): 586–600.
2 Grant, A. M. Coaching for enhanced performance. Comparing cognitive and behavioural coaching approaches. Paper presented at the 3rd Spearman Conference, Sydney, Australia.

3   Carver, C. S. and Scheier, M. F. *On the Self-regulation of Behaviour*. 1998. Cambridge: Cambridge University Press.
4   Van de Walle, D., Brown, S. P., Cron, W. L. and Slocum, J. W. Jr. The influence of goal orientation and self-regulation tactics on sales performance: a longitudinal field test. *Journal of Applied Psychology*. 1999, **84**(2): 249–59.
5   Locke, E. A. Motivation through conscious goal setting. *Applied and Preventive Psychology*. 1999, **5**(2): 117–24.
6   Showers. C. and Cantor, N. Social cognition: a look at motivated strategies. *Annual Review of Psychology*. 1985, **36**: 275–305.

chapter four

1   Toffler, A. *Business Minds* by Tom Brown, Stuart Crainer, Des Dearlove and Jorge Rodrigues is a compilation of interviews published by Financial Times Prentice Hall, 2002.
2   Gallwey, T. *The Inner Game of Work*, Texere Publishing Ltd, p. 3.
3   Bridges, W. *Managing Transitions: Making the Most of Change*. 1991. London: Nicholas Brealey.
4   Prochaska, J. O. and DiClemente, C. Strong and weak principles for progressing from precontemplation to action on the basis of twelve problem behaviors. *Health Psychology*. 1994, **13**(1): 47 51.
5   Prochaska, J. O., Norcross, J. C. and DiClemente, C. C. Stages of change and decisional balance for 12 problem behaviors. Avon Books (Pap Trd); Reprint edition (September 1995). *Health Psychology*. 1994, **13**(1): 39–46.

chapter six

1   Whitmore, J. *Coaching for Performance*. 1992. London: Nicholas Brealey.
2   Egan, G. *The Skilled Helper*. 1974. Pacific Grove, CA: Brooks / Cole Publishing Co.
3   Neale, V. et al. The use of behavioral contracting to increase exercise activity. *American Journal of Health Promotion*. 1990, **4**(6): 441–47.
4   Meillier, L. K., Lund, A. B. and Kok, G. Cues to action in the process of changing lifestyle. *Patient Education and Counseling*. 1997, **30**(1): 37–51.
5   Murtada, N. and Haccoun, R. R. Self-monitoring and goal setting as determinants of the transfer of applied training. *Canadian Journal of Behavioral Science*. 1996, **28**(2): 92–101.

6 Cohen, S. L. and Jaffee, C. L. Managing human performance for productivity. *Training and Development Journal*. 1982, **36**(12): 94–100.

7 Scherer, R. F. et al. Identification of managerial behavior dimensions in a federal health-care agency. *Psychological Reports*. 1995, **76**(2): 675–9.

8 Beck, A. et al. *Cognitive Therapy of Depression*. 1979. New York: Guildford Press.

9 Erickson. M. H. and Rossi, E. L. Varieties of double bind. *American Journal of Clinical Hypnosis*. 1975, **17**(3): 143–57.

chapter seven

1 Toffler, A. *Business Minds* by Tom Brown, Stuart Crainer, Des Dearlove and Jorge Rodrigues is a compilation of interviews published by Financial Times Prentice Hall, 2002.

chapter nine

1 Kelly, P. J. Coach the coach. *Training and Development Journal*. 1985, **39**(11): 54–5.

2 Butler, G. et al. Comparison of behavior therapy and cognitive behavior therapy in the treatment of generalized anxiety disorder. *Journal of Consulting and Clinical Psychology*. 1991, **59**(1): 167–75.

3 Evered, R. D. and Selman, J. C. Coaching and the art of management. *Organizational Dynamics*. 1989, **18**(2): 16–32.

4 Strayer, J. and Rossett, A. Coaching sales performance: a case study. *Performance Improvement Quarterly*. 1994, **7**(4): 39–53.

5 Mace, M. L. The growth and development of executives. 1950. Boston: Harvard Business School, Division of Research.

6 Wyld, B. Expert push. *Sydney Morning Herald*. 2001: 4.

7 Barber, J. Coaching: a human capital solution for improving workforce performance. *Behavioral Healthcare Tomorrow*. 2001, **10**(2): SR29.

8 Wageman, R. Critical success factors for creating superb self-managing teams. *Organizational Dynamics*. 1997, **26**(1): 49–61.

9 Gold, M., van Gelder, M. and Schalock, R. L. A behavioral approach to understanding and managing organizational change: moving from worship to community employment. *Journal of Rehabilitation Administration*. 1999, **22**(3): 191–207.

10 Wissbrun, D. L. The reduction of managerial stress through skilled development in performance counseling and performance coaching. *Dissertation Abstracts International*. 1984, **44**(12-A): 3571–72.

11 Konczak, L. J., Stelly, D. J. and Trusty, M. L. Defining and measuring empowering leader behaviors: development of an upward feedback instrument. *Educational and Psychological Measurement*. 2000, **60**(2): 301–13.

12 Manzoni, J. A better way to deliver bad news. *Harvard Business Review*. 2002, September: 4–8.

13 Latham, G. P. Establishment of goals, feedback and motivation of the industrial employee. *Revista Interamericana de Psicologia Ocupacional*. 1985, **4**(3): 37–41.

notes

solution-focused coaching

momentum

index